Acknowledgements: I am indebted to Carole and Joseph Keating for editorial assistance and for suggestions in typographical layout to Arthur Howe.

Book design by William Berchen.

First published in 1975 by Houghton Mifflin Company, Boston, Massachusetts 02107

Library of Congress catalogue card number 74-32403

ISBN 0-395-19418-0

Printed and bound in Italy by Mondadori Editore, Verona.

aspects of Boston

William Berchen

Text by
Ursula and William Berchen

HOUGHTON MIFFLIN COMPANY   BOSTON   1975

Introduction

The purpose of this photographic essay is to convey the visual impact of Boston as it is now; but this leaves, as always, the problem of the pages between the pictures.

Should we talk about the photographs? That might just end up as redundant drivel, for they make their own statement. Should we go through the endless litany of the crushing urban problems afflicting Boston, as they do all our cities? That would just leave us in the doldrums, and it is certainly not the intent of this book to lift lids on urban garbage pails. Perhaps the best direction this text can take is to describe some of the conditions of the very hard-working world of early Boston, which, after all, is the essence of what helped to give this city in American history (to paraphrase Lewis Mumford) its present form. Many kinds of work built Boston, whether by tradesman, craftsman, housewife, merchant, or laborer; whatever the motivation, from basic life support to the expression of philosophical, aesthetic, political, or commercial ideals.

To understand more fully the distance traveled in the quality of our urban life we might find it profitable to look at how earlier generations of our townspeople lived. For this purpose we are going to avail ourselves of figures like Thomas Hancock, Paul Revere, and others, not to write anything resembling biographies of these august historical personages, but only to make use of them as pivotal figures, and as a framework in which to place a picture of their times.

In these descriptions of everyday life we hope to convey an inkling of what it must have been like to pursue one's livelihood in Boston in the century of our Revolution, and in doing so, we can use the contrasts to contemplate the fortunes and failures of urban life in Boston today.

Public Garden at Arlington Street

Much in Common

Walk through the red-brick, carefully formed harmony of Boston's older architecture and streets, its malls, parks, and esplanades, through the baroque decoration of its late nineteenth and early twentieth century commercial sections, through the cold impressiveness of Modern Monumental, as well as through the sleaze of Unrestricted Commercial (which is of great interest in its own way), and you will see the symbols of roads we have traveled in our history, and the signs of the direction we might be taking now.

Boston, not overwhelmed as yet by the twentieth century, may be the American city that can still give us insight into the meaning of our urban evolution. Here the past is still clearly visible in the present, and the intent of its beginning can still be felt. For after all, it is the city where our Revolutionary hopes began.

In Boston, to breathe the air is still possible, to escape the worst traffic is still possible, and, given reasonably healthy legs and feet, to cover the essence of this city on foot is still possible. And what better place to start than on the Common, which has been there since the town's beginning, and is likely to be with us to the very end?

The Common was still a large, rough field in the 1830's, abundant with wildflowers to be picked by the basketful. There were hardly any trees until later, when orderly walks were laid out, and the rough surfaces smoothed over. Today the Common has the feel of a refuge, but always one within a city, as there is never quite enough insulation from intrusive sounds of traffic at the edges. But we are grateful that, amidst the noise, dirt, and confusion of our modern city, Boston Common is one of the few oases to provide softer surfaces for the senses.

The nostalgic image of an English common is of a grazing ground, personifying the old-world pastoral scene, with cows, sheep, horses, and a donkey, the only sounds being those of birds twittering in the hedge, and the animals wrenching up mouthfuls of grass, while routine village life meanders peacefully on at the perimeter.

One would have to go back quite a way in time to recapture much of that atmosphere on Boston Common; and yet the Common has always been there, as a focus of communal life, since the time that the town was first settled in 1630, when the transplanted East Anglians took a tentative hold on their new surroundings, and began to wrest a semblance of their far-away home from the alien wilderness of New England. But Boston Common was no neat meadow, such as they may have been used to, surrounded by trees and hedges, with each distant village indicated by the glimpse of an occasional spire. Instead, there was open country running down to the harbor, with a pasture below some hills; and for people who clambered to the tops, a view of a great expanse of wild country, with lakes, rivers, and more hills, and little sign of human habitation except the etched lines of a few Indian tracks. The peninsula, then known as Shawmut, was irregularly shaped, and attached to the mainland by a skinny neck that was awash at high tide, and had a lot of salt marshes and mud flats at the edges. Not a propitious beginning for the hub of New England!

One of the first items to be taken care of in the new settlement was the choice of a site for grazing ground and a military training field, as the fledgling community lived in fear of the Indians who also needed clear land, which was scanty in this rock-bedeviled region. (Ironically, many of the Indians, under the double threat of sickness and attack by stronger tribes, put themselves under the protection of the newcomers.)

Boston's first English settler was the Reverend William Blaxton, who settled on Shawmut in 1625, near a spring on the western slope of Trimountain, whose lopped-off form we know as Beacon Hill. He built himself a house and for five years this studious, self-sufficient cleric lived alone with his orchard, vegetables, flowers, and books. When his fellow countrymen arrived he was sympathetic and helpful, but found the intensity of their continuing company tiresome. (After all, that was why he had left East Anglia in the first place.) In 1634 he resettled, but further afield. Apparently though, all his needs were not met by books and plants, as he returned to Boston some years later to marry a widow.

Before he moved away the town had bought most of his land, six shillings being extracted from each householder, and for two hundred years these forty-odd acres were the military training field and communal pasture. For the first ten years part of the Common was also the site of the dump, an excrescence that evidently did not cause any furor. There was no health department, but there was an order requiring every householder to keep the street clean in front of his dwelling and to dispose of the rubbish. The farmers who brought provisions in from the country were hired to carry away the offal and sweepings. These countrymen, naturally being disinclined to take the refuse any further than they had to, unloaded the stuff in the obvious place—the Common—where it could be shared by all, along with the pleasanter aspects. There have always been plenty of people who think that the countryside is largely for rubbish disposal; now there are millions, with the manufacturers to abet them. In mid-seventeenth century a twenty-shilling fine was imposed for spreading trash on the Common; what a pity we cannot catch the culprits in the twentieth, even with all our clever gadgets for minding each other's business. In spite of this fine the Tremont Street Mall became an extended dump from one end to the other, but at least the contents were biodegradable, and perhaps the colonial seagulls grew to be nearly as big as albatrosses, the way they do today at country dumps.

Records for 1646 show that seventy "milch kine" and just one horse were allowed on Boston Common. The privileged horse belonged to Elder Thomas Oliver, a physician, and it was to remain by special act of legislature because the congregation of the First Church liked their Deacon. Also, he needed his horse to make his rounds, that being long before the sick were expected to drag themselves to the doctor's office, where they must share their germs and distresses with the other patients. Of course, the likelihood of curing any serious illness was rather remote, and upon due consideration the colder, clinical efficiency of today's medical science is preferable.

Seventeenth century citizenry took military duty for granted. All adult males with, as usual, the exclusion of some office holders, were members of the Artillery Company, based on London's "Ancient and Honourable Artillery Company." Fines were levied for not attending the drilling sessions, for being late, or for forgetting one's weapon. The fine money went toward banners, drums, or other military material, but the town was also required to maintain a watch house, produce saltpeter, and keep a store of weapons and gunpowder. Like raw recruits anywhere, some of the men were clumsy, careless, argumentative, or hopelessly inept, and there was a relaxed attitude toward discipline that would be all too familiar to an exasperated modern drill sergeant, but somehow they did manage to look after Boston. Their town duties consisted of chasing "Murtherers, Manslayers, Peace-breakers, Theevs, Robbers, Burglarers," and they could, without a warrant, catch drunks, liars, vagrants, and Sabbath breakers. Mothers were not to caress their children on Sunday, nor husbands to kiss their wives. A great many things were forbidden on the Sabbath, including idleness, so people could not just sit and twiddle their thumbs, but they could always fall back on reading the Bible.

When they were not fulfilling their military or civic duties these Bostonians were average artisans, laborers, farmers, or merchants, and must have spent much of their scanty free time on the Common, since that was where most of the interesting things went on. One can imagine a diorama containing a great variety of activities, as between the seventeenth century and the present day there have been: skating on the frog pond, coasting, dueling, lovers' meetings, political meetings, antislavery meetings, and revival meetings. The Common was the place to air clothes after a smallpox epidemic, or to gather after a devastating fire. It was from the foot of the Common that the British embarked for their journey along the Charles to what was to become the battle of Lexington; and it was on the Common that they were encamped during the siege of Boston. Cold and discouraged, they planted and tended their own vegetables to eke out the meagre food supply.

For excitement there have been horse racing, balloon ascending, kite flying, hoop rolling, fireworks, and spinning contests. (A spinning school, supported by public funds, was instituted early in the town's settlement, as a vital part of a self-sustaining community.) For further entertainment people could hurl abuse, filth, and rotten fruit at the humiliated victims of the pillory, stocks, or whipping post. A special ordeal was often meted out to horse thieves, whose session at the whipping post was prefaced by a spell on the "wooden horse," a simple chunk of wood, mounted on four legs, whose riders could cover their embarrassment by clowning for the spectators. The missiles flew just the same, and justice, or at any rate punishment, was carried out with Draconian swiftness.

And of course there was the gallows. Erected in 1644 as yet another adjunct to colonial life, it saw the dispatch of over a hundred people, from Quakers to pirates, before it was moved to a less conspicuous place in 1812, still to be used, but no longer considered so suitable for public entertainment. The seventeenth century was not troubled by squeamishness, and spectators wearing their best clothes arrived in the thousands by boat, on horseback, and on foot to watch some wretch be "turned off." Judge Sewall, that invaluable diarist, tells us that on a day when seven pirates were hanged, his wife could hear the women screeching, from her orchard a mile away. Many condemned were used, in those days, as awful examples, since it was too late for them to mend their ways, and for weeks before their execution they were chained and handcuffed and dragged in carts to public meetings, where ministers righteously held forth about the criminals' sins.

As Puritans were denied games, dancing, the theater, and sports, they turned to amusements that seem weird to us; but although we no longer condone eye-gouging, ear-cropping, tongue-slitting, or public executions of humans, there are a great number of people who accept cruelty to animals, in the world of so-called sports, ranging from unthinking callousness to deliberate sadism. In our art, movies, and literature, there is a preoccupation with cruelty to humans that is discouraging, and that may point to truths hidden within us all.

In an age when even children could be hanged for stealing a pocket handkerchief, it is not surprising that a bonnet, worth a trifling sum, was the undoing of one woman, who snatched it from its owner, who was carrying it on her arm. Poor Rachel Wall! Perhaps there was someone special she hoped to impress at church the following Sunday. Or did she have a sudden mad urge to borrow a bit of finery? The world over, headgear denotes the rank or position of the wearer: fireman, soldier, Indian chief, milkmaid, or Skid Row bum. Perhaps Rachel had been eyeing that bonnet for days, and had an irresistible desire to look like a lady of fashion.

Once when another woman, a murderess, was hanged on the Common, she delighted the crowd by appearing in a white dress. Cotton Mather "was scandalized at the hussy's effrontery" when she remained unimpressed by his sermon, and even more so when she stole the limelight by bowing and smiling to the onlookers. Was her composure due to the resilience of her ego, or to the potency of "rumm"?

As a comfort in pain and adversity, as a reward for hard work, and as a beverage safer than water, rum was a necessity of life. Living as we do now in one of the world's greatest medical centers, with doctors, antibiotics, and pain killers within reach of most (though at a price), we cannot imagine how it must have been to go through sickness, bungled surgery, and primitive dentistry without the talents and comforts that we rely on. Bostonians currently rank among the nation's most excessive drinkers and to the city's forebears rum was a major item in the development of international trade; millions of gallons were distilled and exported annually from the town in the eighteenth century, much of it destined for barter in the slave trade. But a huge quantity was consumed in the town itself and was a major factor in the development of the respectable paunch that, with a portrait by Smibert or Copley, was proof of a businessman's success.

If public hangings were a form of justice, though there is grave doubt as to their deterrent value, there were also the more private and ritualistic duels, demanded to assuage the slighted egos of the times. Peter Faneuil's nephew, Benjamin Phillips, fought one on the Common in 1728 over a love affair, under the mammoth 'Old Elm,' the tree that was large when Winthrop came to settle Boston, but that succumbed to a severe storm in 1876. Phillips' opponent also succumbed, so we hope it was Phillips that the young lady wanted. As a result of this encounter a stringent law was passed against dueling, but the custom may have continued covertly, as it certainly flourished until much later in other parts of the country. The common brawl was unseemly for gentlemen; and yet how else was one to redress one's stained reputation but by a duel for which one had received training and discipline of mind and body, to be brought to the test upon a "field of honor," where the loss incurred might be anything from a life to a fingertip?

But far and away the greater number of scenes enacted on Boston's Common have been pleasurable, and it is a great place for special celebrations. In 1837, when Queen Victoria ascended the British throne, there was a spectacular show by Indians, complete with war paint and feather headdresses, doing dances before a crowd of thousands. Annually the Fourth of July provided an even greater justification, and with country fair atmosphere: booths, merry-go-rounds, barkers, and from fifteen to twenty thousand people having a good and exhausting time all day, waiting for the band concert in the evening. In 1848 a very special celebration took place on the Common for the introduction of Cochituate Water into Boston. The beginning of modern plumbing was indeed something to celebrate, and Boston was making progress, as bathtubs had been prohibited until 1842 as a menace to health!

Ever since mankind became aware of himself and his neighbors, people-watching must have been a popular pastime. For this fascinating occupation Boston Common has its benches, though wooden ones were replaced with iron ones in the nineteenth century, to discourage whittling. (Now we have wooden ones back again.) If the old ones had remained it might have been interesting to speculate about some of our forebears' examples of "primitive art." Most of us deplore the surge of vandalism that has occurred in recent years. Is it caused by the population growth that engenders an increasing anonymity for the individual who now feels compelled to leave a symbol of his existence, or is it the product of frustration, rage, or both? But looking at fifteenth century initials carved on a recumbent figure in a European church, we feel more curiosity about the disrespectful carver than resentment, and most grateful that spray paint had not yet been invented. Evidently, present-day affronts are much harder to forgive. But whatever our destructive compulsions, we must not dig up sods from the Common! This was long ago forbidden, since the Common was "the beauty and pride of the Town, ever suggesting the lighter side of life."

If you agree that the lighter side of life should carry the most weight, linger for as long as you can on the Common. For the Common today is a delight. Clement weather brings out the pigeon feeders, who sustain that remarkable species that has made the coziest adjustment to man and urban life—no sign of extinction here. The damage caused by his freely spattered acid droppings is small payment for the marvel of his coral eyes and feet, the mechanical-toy walk, and the explosion of beating wings in the pigeon-swarm at the feeding corner of Park and Tremont Streets. What is this urge to feed pigeons? Is it a gratification that comes from feeding dependent life, without danger of any permanent attachment? Is it the rarity of such an easily spooked creature as a bird gripping your arm for a branch and taking food from your hand, inducing a few seconds of oneness with nature? Are the little old men and women who feed pigeons as a daily ritual reassured by these living beings, perhaps the last to show some reliance on them?

The Common is of course filled with other varieties of wondrous fauna: shoppers resting their feet, office workers basking and eating their lunches, Skid Row snoozers, and others better heeled, stretched out on the grass, lovers, as closely wrapped as the public will allow, troubadours playing for money, troubadours playing for love, and some for both; briefcased men in stride between one appointment and the next, prepared to buy, sell, or litigate (there is a parking garage under the Common, and it is very civilized to exit from your car into a walk in the park before being swallowed up by concrete.) In summer the frog pond effervesces with children who shriek with pleasure in daring dashes into the fountain fall in the center, watched by indulgent mothers who have escaped the confinement of four walls, and by loungers in the shaded grass who view it all with a gentle nostalgia. In winter the snow is etched by the sharp lines of the trees, and the air by the squeak of blades, bringing to mind a scene by Breughel.

All this continuing life flows over the Common, much as it always has, but enhanced by a fine aspect that is to be found in relatively few other American cities, since the lovely brick borders of the Beacon and Park Street buildings have been affectionately left undisturbed, in belated appreciation of our eighteenth and nineteenth century heritage.

Of course, we do not imply that all modern planning and construction is a disturbance, though it all too often is. We appreciate the best in the new urban landscape, providing it does not swallow or overwhelm the old. After all, the rawness of the new, if it has any inherent worth, will achieve in time the patina and charm of the old.

The Common was necessary to our beginning, and it is even more essential to our present, for the proportion of Boston that the Common represented two hundred years ago was infinitely larger than the share that it has of today's urbanscape, and we suspect that the psychological necessity for its refuge is stronger than it ever has been. Though in Boston we have more green than many American cities, it doesn't mean that we have enough. When and if we can better manage our population, our social dislocations, our clotted traffic, our urban renewal, and architectural conservation—in short, if the city with time becomes more controllable rather than less—we will perhaps see every obsolete parking lot, dump, and piece of urban decay turning into a common.

The Common from Park Street

Commonwealth Avenue Mall

◄ *Colonel Prescott, Bunker Hill*

View from the Athenaeum

Pounds, Shillings, and Pence

Walking around present-day Boston and seeing the considerable number of impregnable fortresses for the safekeeping of MONEY, one can feel either reassured or intimidated, according to one's means and temperament. We in the twentieth century find it difficult to imagine a society in which hard cash was extremely rare, and in which there were no banks at all, but Boston did not have its first bank until 1784; and even then the policies were conservative and the investments local, until after the Civil War, when railroads changed the face of the earth, as well as the outlook of the city fathers. Thomas Hancock, who founded one of New England's largest fortunes, would have been delighted to see the results of his labors, and astonished to hear the bouncy radio and TV jingles that now exhort us to borrow, and to save, with equal coziness.

Thomas Hancock? He was not only John's uncle, but was also the first American business tycoon. Since the thirteenth century days of mercantile capitalism there had been, in addition to the traveling merchant, the stay-at-home merchant who was the kingpin of the whole economic system. Thomas apparently never went anywhere much, but from the House of Hancock, near the wharves of Boston, he exerted considerable influence on the sustenance and development of the New England colony, and with his canny manipulations kept it on its financial feet during many of the pre-Revolutionary years.

Although Thomas managed his business and made policy decisions mainly for his own profit, he also aimed to construct a stronger Boston, and to develop resources in the hinterland. He found supplies for produce, did some banking, some mining, and promoted the local manufacture of ships, paper, and potash; he played a large part in the whaling industry; he bought considerable New England real estate; and no war could have been fought without him. With his kind of help Boston eventually changed through the years from being a satellite of London into a busy metropolis with its own factories, railroads, and banks.

Commerce during the colonial era was interwoven with smuggling, privateering, expeditions against the French, settlement of the frontier, and patching up the military outposts of Empire. If anyone has wondered who planned the smuggling trips and financed the privateers, or how General Wolfe got the scanty rations of biscuits and pickled pork for his redcoats, it was because the firm of Hancock was behind it all, pulling the strings. Although always varied and far-reaching, business affairs in the Hancock establishment were rather mild between wars, as peace provided relatively meagre pickings. But with Jenkins' Ear, King George's War, and the French and Indian Wars there were intermittent hostilities for more than twenty years to raise Thomas' profits, and his spirits. However regrettable a war might be, it was a chance not to be sneezed at when the mother country was ready to spend money in the colonies, and Thomas was equally ready to rail against the enemy of the moment and to twitch the threads that connected him with his overseas agents, entreating them to send him supplies such as homespun, shoes, stockings, wheat, transport, equipment, gunpowder, or whatever was needed. He became remarkably resourceful, and although he was not very scrupulous in his methods, he managed to trade in everything, from salt to feathers, to keep the flow of goods coming in to the New England colonies.

Entrance, Public Garden
City Hall Plaza

During the first half of the eighteenth century a well-organized monetary system was rare anywhere in the world, but in New England the confusion was phenomenal. Price levels seesawed wildly; paper money was blithely printed up, at frequent intervals, as New England was without coins of her own. Most people never handled cash, and businessmen did so only rarely. What monies they did come by originated from a great variety of countries, and were sent to England to pay business debts. When a British general left his luggage with Thomas for safekeeping and fell overboard near Boston, his baggage was found to contain an assortment of joannes, moidores, pistoles, guineas, gold, "small heart" bits of silver, a dollar and a ha'penny. But with all the expertise he had acquired in his counting house no doubt Thomas was able to calculate the equivalent in pounds, shillings, and pence—Massachusetts style, that is, which had different values from their British counterparts.

Generally, money units were used for reckoning only, as, with scanty cash and unstable banknotes, trade in New England was mostly carried on by an ingenious form of barter, based on debit and credit. Simple barter would soon have brought trade to a standstill, so a system of negotiation was needed in which goods and services were either used in direct payment of debt, or were reassigned by the creditor to someone else to whom he was indebted. In this way materials and craft work went hither and yon, both on paper and in fact, records of the times showing fish to have been the most traveled item. As had been established in the early days of Boston's settlement, debts were discharged by means of eggs, corn, chickens, hogs, or vegetables; but this "country pay" had to be as-

sessed promptly, and either soon eaten up, or disposed of to someone else. Quick thinking was needed if the payment was standing at the door, on the hoof, as to whether it should be kept, fed and housed, until a more propitious time, or used as a means of immediate exchange. There must have been times when a creditor saw no ready use for the proffered goods, as, for example, a pair of wrought iron gates, so they would be set aside for some future opportunity. (Did colonial wives grumble about "all that rubbish you keep out in the back"?) No doubt the local merchants had their fingers on the pulse of the community, and, like businessmen of all time, while talking shop in the local tavern made mental notes as to who might be able to use what. An intriguing variety of goods changed hands: Thomas Hancock's father-in-law, a book seller, paid a carpenter for repair work not only with books, but also with wood, a gun, cider, barrels of beef, pencils, candles, hogs, and molasses.

In 1716, when Thomas came from his father's Lexington parsonage to Boston, as a lad of scarcely fourteen, he found a market town of some fourteen thousand inhabitants, which was not only the seat of the General Court and the Royal Governor, but was also North America's chief business center, and the main link between Britain and her American colonies. As in the seventeenth century, Boston imported large amounts of goods from England, to whom she was always in debt, in exchange for what New England had to offer.

Although New England's stony soil could not produce a great deal that England wanted, the seas were lush in comparison. By 1730 the whaling industry had been developed into a systematic slaughter, with Nantucket as the chief whaling center and Boston as the main market and distribution point, while the whaling grounds expanded far into the North Atlantic, as Newfoundland became more settled. Although whale oil was greatly in demand, the crews got little or no regular pay, receiving instead a substantial share of the value of the catch, in proportion to their rank.

Thomas Hancock, and later his nephew John, bought large amounts of oil and whalebone to send to London (on one trip the whalebone even had to be stacked in the cabins). Whalebone was actually a "conglomeration of hairs covered with enamel-like fibrous tissue," and when appropriately treated yielded strong, flexible strips that were used extensively for fans, carriage tops, corsets, helmets, and carriage whips. (In the following century twenty million whips were turned out each year in Westfield, Massachusetts.)

Another item that was exported in tremendous amounts was that old standby, rum. When Newfoundland was still a fledgling outpost five thousand gallons at a time were distilled in Boston and sent up there, to keep out the cold and help with the work at hand. Great quantities were also sent to Africa, in exchange for slaves, who were shipped from there to the West Indies; and from there molasses for the New England rum industry completed the heinous triangle. Thomas owned a number of ships, and was involved in some very dubious transactions of his own, but there is no evidence that he traded in slaves, though he had a few in his household. In the 1750's there were about three thousand blacks in Massachusetts, most of them in the Boston area, but there was a strong feeling against slavery in New England. There was a duty on every black imported into the colony, and to free a slave cost the former owner up to fifty pounds to the town treasurer, to ensure the freed slave would not become a public charge. Hostile Indians, however, were sold as slaves, and this was considered acceptable.

When Thomas arrived from the country he was at first apprenticed for the customary seven years, like his contemporaries Ben Franklin and Apollos Rivoire—Paul Revere's father. Thomas went to live with Samuel Gerrish, a bookseller, for whom he would run errands, sell quills, and bind sermons. He was to obey the Gerrishes, keep their secrets, warn them of evil-doers, and not waste their goods. "Matrimony he shall not contract, Taverns and Alehouses he shall not frequent, at cards, dice, or any other unlawful games he shall not play." Apprentices, in this country and in Europe, earned the reputation of being holy terrors, but they worked very long hours, and were naturally more than ready to explode into mischief and vandalism when they were let out. As they were required to learn their skills thoroughly, from the consumers' point of view there is much to recommend the old system of training. In return for Thomas' model behavior he learned the skill of bookbinding and got his meat, drink and lodging, and Mrs. Gerrish saw that his clothes were washed. No wages were mentioned in the agreement.

At twenty-one he set up his own business, at the sign of the Bible and Three Crowns, on Anne (now North) Street, a stone's throw from the harbor, as it was then, before being filled in. Even when Ben Franklin established a lending library in Philadelphia, Boston had the only good bookshop in the colonies, for in New York, as well as Philadelphia, the printers were just stationers who sold paper, almanacs, ballads, and a few school books. Thomas worked hard at publishing and selling books, which were mainly in the uplifting category; one had the particularly snappy title of "The Danger of People's Losing the Good Impressions made by the late awful Earthquake."

Due to the great diversity of goods that Thomas had to take in exchange for his books, he was bound to become the owner of a general store. When he died in 1764, an advertisement for the store began "Store No. 4 at east end of Faneuil Market, a general assortment of English and India Goods, also Choice Newcastle Coals, and Irish Butter cheap for Cash." Two thirds of the store were taken up with the dress department, which sounds familiar, and it included cloth, ribbons, knee and shoe buckles, hatbands, and fans. In the hardware department there were compasses, fire steels, hourglasses, larding pins, and swords. Provisions included tea, coal, ship's stores, salt, leather, lime, and the indispensible rum. In fact the store was the equivalent of the modern mail-order house, with the backbone of its trade being the country trader with his basket on his arm, who made a convenient outlet for goods that were not too successful among the more sophisticated Bostonians. The postal service was still very spotty. Mail carriers fitted it in with delivering oxen, or whatever; one of them used to knit on the way, and they all used to read—and spread—the news that they were carrying, unless code or seals were used. Very possibly some postmen even mastered these special challenges. So to get his orders delivered with some reliability Thomas had them carried by the chapmen, or peddlars, who all came to Boston on a regular basis. There was a constant flow of goods from Boston outwards to the developing towns inland and along the seaboard. The first stage was by small coastal or river boats, then the goods were transferred to pack animal, and often ended their journey on a pushcart. Then the flow was reversed, and produce, fish, chickens and hogs were brought back by land and water to the hub. Credit was vital, often running over many months, or even years, in spite of failure to pay meaning compound interest. But Thomas was, in some respects, just as bad at paying off his own debts. Some of them were still unpaid nineteen years after his death.

Although he was a skinflint and must have been hated for some of his methods of providing capital, provide it he did, for many ventures. One of his early ones was for New England's first paper factory, whose chief partner was Daniel Henchman. An old fulling mill was found eight miles away on the Neponset River, at a location that is now in Milton, where the tides were used for power. The foreman was English, with two or three boys under him. As modern bleaching methods were unknown, good paper had to be made from select rags, which were advertised for in the Henchman and Hancock bookstores, but were in short supply, probably due to a combination of Yankee thrift and the climate not encouraging the wearing of linen. Some of the needed rags even had to be imported from England. But once procured, and at a price, the rags were hand-shredded on a scythe attached to a post, and then turned into pulp by a water-driven device consisting of rollers that ran over a plate covered with knives, or ridges. The pulp was then molded into sheets, which were pressed and hung in the loft; pressed and hung again; and then trimmed. All of this was done by hand, took about three months, and in the process every sheet would be handled separately six times. By the end of each fifteen-hour work day perhaps sixty pounds of paper were produced. Statistics like these are a reproach to all of us twentieth century paper squanderers, and we can see why our ancestral clergymen wrote out their interminable sermons in such miniscule handwriting. The mill prospered, but not enough to cause anxiety to the British government, which kept a wary eye on American industries, for fear of too brisk competition.

Boston's waterfront is a relatively quiet place these days, but not so very long ago it teemed with activity. In Thomas' time the harbor was alive with merchant ships, whalers, ferries, and fishing boats, with an extra spurt of life in the spring. (As an added attraction there were seals in the harbor, but their descendants finally abandoned the area about forty years ago. They couldn't stomach the water any more.) Long Wharf, now obliterated in State Street, was the busiest landing place, and a remarkable structure for the times, as it ran for over two thousand feet into the water, and was big enough to allow the world's largest ships to come alongside. Over five hundred ships a year cleared the port, and since there were no steam tugs, vessels of all sizes sailed in and out of the harbor under full sail.

All this waterfront animation was accommodated by auction halls, warehouses, counting houses, sail lofts, markets, taverns, and shops. Pungent and varied smells proclaimed "land" to the long-at-sea crews, and a discerning nose would be able to identify the assorted aromas and stinks of bread, rum, dyes, offal, tar, fish, sewage, coffee, leather, horses, coal, and cattle. Some sound effects would consist of dogs barking, cattle lowing, horses whinnying, seagulls lamenting, peddlars crying, pulleys squeaking, canvas flapping, rigging slapping, and the long-awaited goods thudding on the dock. The tempo of the business day was set by the arrival of the large ships, and when one was expected handbills were distributed, the bulk of the advertising aimed, as always, at the ladies. When the elegant sails were sighted the action was intensified. From the counting houses came elaborately dressed merchants, their prosperity well in evidence, for the eighteenth century Puritan was no advocate of sad-colored garments; local girls and boys kept their eyes open, the former for sailors, and the latter for the privilege of running an errand, as the boys were very familiar with the waterfront. The black stevedores were ready to do their back-breaking job of hauling up the cargo from the hold, with block and tackle, singing as they worked. When winches were later introduced, blacks were no longer seen on Boston's wharves.

There was a pecking order in the world of sail, and if a humble fishing smack approached the wrong dock, she would be told, in no uncertain terms, to get out. The merchant's warehouse and counting house were where his ships came in and he supervised their loading and unloading; in this way each wharf had its own characters and characteristics. The merchants continued the seventeenth century custom of meeting to exchange news at the Town House, now the Old State House, and were said to meet "on 'change." This place became known as the Royal Exchange, and the local tavern and lane were named after it.

There was always a likelihood of loss for an importer. Fire was an ever-present threat; goods were of poor quality, or badly packed and therefore damaged. Vinegar leaked; tea and coffee became inextricably intermingled; "ratts" ate books (the umpteenth generation of their descendants, being no respecters of persons, is now annoying the occupants of the very expensive apartments on Boston's waterfront, where flotsam and jetsam still slop against the sea wall.) The use of ice as a preservative, and as a cargo itself, did not come about until the early eighteen hundreds, when another talented and persistent Bostonian, Frederick Tudor, "The Ice King," started what became a very profitable world-wide venture. He persevered in spite of his business associates thinking him mad, and his first crews thinking their ships would be swamped by melting ice. There is a memorial to him in the little garden beside the Old North Church.

But if Thomas Hancock found some of his shipments of pork were rotten, or if beer "stunk" or was "mustey" or "sower," he often "innocently" rerouted them to another unsuspecting victim, and relayed their deplorable condition to Christopher Kilby, his London agent, with insurance claims in mind. Accidents happened, even though one of the ruses Thomas employed was to have government goods stashed on deck, exposed to all weathers, while his own were safely stowed in the hold! All voyages were very slow, resulting not only in spoiled foodstuffs, but in general ignorance of world affairs, and providing convenient excuses for alibis and procrastination. Britain's extensive and irksome restrictions on shipping and trade were another challenge to be circumnavigated, although policies made in far-off London, and intended to govern both countries, were not of immediate concern to most New Englanders, who, like average people anywhere, were engrossed in their daily lives. Laws that did not suit could often be evaded, while the colonial authorities looked the other way; and when a loophole was found the New Englanders succumbed to the temptation with alacrity. Thomas set up a very successful illicit trade with

Surinam, which became notorious for smuggling, meanwhile constraining his captains to secrecy, and devising a number of "schems" to fool the authorities.

Among other business hazards were periodic bouts of smallpox, and Thomas was one of the few advocates of inoculation. Letters had to be smoked to free them from the germs; ports and newly recovered passengers were shunned; debts were likely to remain unpaid because an outbreak had caused an exodus into the countryside (though townspeople were not welcomed there), from whence some did not return, having either settled or died. French privateers caused goods and letters to go astray and insurance rates to rise. Sailors were "cruel hard" to find in Boston because of press gangs, and those who escaped demanded high wages. Jealousy from rival merchants had to be outmaneuvered, debts to British suppliers fretted over, ships' captains given their instructions, agents pacified and persuaded.

Up until the end of the Middle Ages, traders usually traveled with their goods and got the best prices possible after reaching their destinations. In the seventeenth century the round trip from Boston to London and back took from three to four months, but as the speed of ships improved, traders were able to stay at home and work by correspondence with their agents, even if it went at a snail's pace. Then when communications speeded up even more in the ninetenth century, the consignment agent became outdated, for as soon as it was feasible to cable buyers in the world's main markets, and to get a price by return, there was no need for sending off a cargo, hoping for the best, and not knowing what price it had fetched until many, many weeks later. But in the eighteenth century not only did everything still travel slowly, but also circumstances tended to change in the time taken by the voyage. In addition, accurate bookkeeping was extremely rare, and traders could have no true knowledge of what went on in the overseas ledgers; so another subsequent improvement, when New England traded with the Far East, was to send along a supercargo—a passenger, or officer with no seagoing duties—who kept an eye on the agents.

In Thomas' time the consignment agent was the keystone to New England's foreign trade and the success of a businessman's ambitions; the more versatile he was, the more valuable, as this was before the age of specialization. Very close relationships developed between Thomas and his agents. For when an agent was discreet, honest, and enterprising, he was of inestimable value and was likely to be entrusted with a great variety of tasks. He might provide transportation and supplies for military expeditions and settlers, or ransom a prisoner, order shoes, gather rent, function as foster father, or work on propaganda against an unpopular law. Business letters bore a more personal touch then, and family news was mixed in with transactions and price lists. When Christopher Kilby went to London he left his daughter in the care of the Hancocks, and Thomas wrote to describe her wedding and then later reported that "She is of a delicate make, her apron strings shorten, and in due time you will be called Grandfather. . ."

The agents, on their side, held the reins, as without them no transactions could be successfully carried out. In London they were "mift" at times at the way Thomas played off one against the other, and so would send him nothing for a while. Cajoling letters would then be dispatched from the Boston office, while wirepulling, bribery and coercion were employed at the Hancock dining table to beguile officials, inducements taking the form of anything from oysters to a housemaid. Thomas was aided and abetted in all this by his young wife, Lydia (the daughter of Daniel Henchman, moving spirit of the paper company), whom Thomas had married when she was sixteen. There was to be much wooing of influential people, up to and including the governor himself, and Lydia proved to be a gracious and friendly hostess.

Trustworthy and resourceful ships' captains were another tremendous help to a tradesman in this era, as they frequently had to do the bargaining in port. As well as a thorough knowledge of all the hundreds of parts in his ship and his navigational skills, his management of the crew, and passengers if any, it was often the captain's responsibility to dispose of the cargo at the best available price; it was also likely that he himself had a financial interest in the vessel. After selling the cargo he had brought, he had to make arrangements for a new one, either to take back home, or to yet another port. Sometimes this might mean weeks of waiting about before a profitable cargo was available, and would also mean hiring a fresh crew; and yet speed was of the essence, since the first cargo to arrive fetched the best price. Spoiled goods were fairly common, and if "oyl" or meat were bad the price would be lower and the market limited.

All the involvements, risks, scares, setbacks, and achievements were, in the long run, life blood to Thomas, as they still are to men who need to manipulate people, goods, and money. With his plump fingers in a great many pies, quite evidently he coped and he and Lydia grew rich fast. By the time he was thirty-two and she was twenty-one they felt it was only just that they keep up with the richer merchants over in London, who were rising rapidly and buying houses in Bloomsbury. In colonial New England there was no false modesty, or nonsense of that sort, about being prosperous and letting it show. Possessions gave evidence that one was approved of by the Almighty: why not be proud of it?

So in 1735—the same year that Paul Revere was born—the shrewd young man picked a bargain tract of well over an acre on Beacon Hill, far from the bustle of Boston, and "with the most beautiful Assent to the Top & its Allowed on all hands the Kingdom of England don't afford so fine a Prospect as I have. . ." There was indeed a "capital prospect" over Boston: over Cambridge with its colleges; over the Charles and Mystic Rivers; south and west to Roxbury, Dorchester Heights, and Brookline; to the Blue Hills of Milton; to Braintree, and over the harbor islands to the lighthouse: a classical colonial panorama.

After a lot of planning, for Thomas was very thorough, a substantial stone house was begun the following year. Anything besides the basic materials had to come from England, so it all took a long, long time, and one can imagine Lydia eagerly awaiting word of the arrival of the expected ships, bearing a hundred-and-one household items for her handsome new home. Thomas sent for window glass (there were fifty-four windows), lamps, three marble hearths, and a ten-foot-high black walnut chiming clock with gilt figures on top. These turned out to be too small. (Had the American love affair with size begun already?) There was paneling, installed with hidden places behind it, and flocked wallpaper. Considerable correspondence seemed to be needed over everything, including the several types of wallpaper. Thomas wanted one kind "very rich & Beautifull fine Cloth" but "well done & as Cheap as Possible" with peacocks, macaws, squirrels, fruits, and "Landskip" at the bottom. After a whole year had elapsed the paper arrived, and was a disappointment.

For the gardens he had enlisted the help of his sea captains, and plants, trees, and fruit trees had come from far and wide. In this respect New England horticulture owes a debt to him and to other wealthy men who set out well-stocked gardens; but he had disappointments even there. He wrote to London, "The trees I Received Last Year are above half Dead;" and "all the seeds . . . (Except the Asparrow grass) was not worth one farthing. Not one of them Came up . . . to Send so far pay dear and be Imposed upon at such a Rate is hard to Bare. . ." Vegetable matter evidently found it even harder than people did to survive the voyage and adapt to Massachusetts soil.

Due to the condition of the roads only the strongest and lightest types of English and Continental carriages were possible, the most popular being the French two-wheeled chaise, which was the ancestor of the buggy. So from London a one-horse chaise was ordered, for Lydia, and a splendid four-horse chariot. These were of course made with pride and conscience, since assembly-line methods were far into the future. Thomas insisted that the chaise be like the one Sir Harry Frankland had bought. Sir Harry was Collector of the Port, and most understanding of the merchants' viewpoint, allowing them to smuggle as they liked with no awkward questions asked. But when Lydia's carriage arrived it was chafed from poor packing, and in "no way equal. . ." But there was an uncommonly low step, since she was a bit weak-kneed, and also "a seat for a boy," who was most likely nephew John Hancock. A coachman was ordered from England too. A coachman with the right presence could give a lot of "tone" to a household, and Thomas stipulated that his should not be an overgrown, fat fellow, nor an old one; and he must understand a kitchen garden. Obviously he was not going to be allowed to hang about the maid servants when he might be making himself useful reassuring those discouraged plants.

In Thomas' day there was a strong affinity between America and the mother country. Pre-Revolutionary Americans had come over from England, or their ancestors had, and both countries dressed alike; at that time they even spoke alike. Several other wealthy Bostonians had decided to end their days impressing "dear London" and Thomas and Lydia considered it, but he was not well, so contented himself with being the wealthiest frog in the expanding pond of Boston. He continued to buy bits and pieces of land, so that by the time he died in 1764 he owned the whole of Beacon Hill, which was fields and orchards remote from the noise and confusion of the town. Anyone hav-

ing a penchant for dolorous subjects might like to figure out the current price of Thomas' property comprising the area within Beacon, Mt. Vernon, Bowdoin, and Joy streets, and compare the cost with what Thomas once paid for it.

The strange thing about Hancock House is, that after being the home of Thomas, then of John and Dolly, and seeing so much elegant life, and being part of American history, it was allowed to deteriorate through one of those baffling civic muddles, and then finally torn down in 1863. Compunction evidently set in, as Massachusetts built a copy of it at the Chicago Exhibition of 1893, but what good did that do Boston? There is a plaque to mark its location, at 25 Beacon Street (which is between numbers 31 and 33, but that is another story.) This is the headquarters of the American Unitarian-Universalist Association, and a handsome house; but how much more satisfactory it would be if the house that Thomas built with such loving care were still keeping an interested eye on the Common and the Hill.

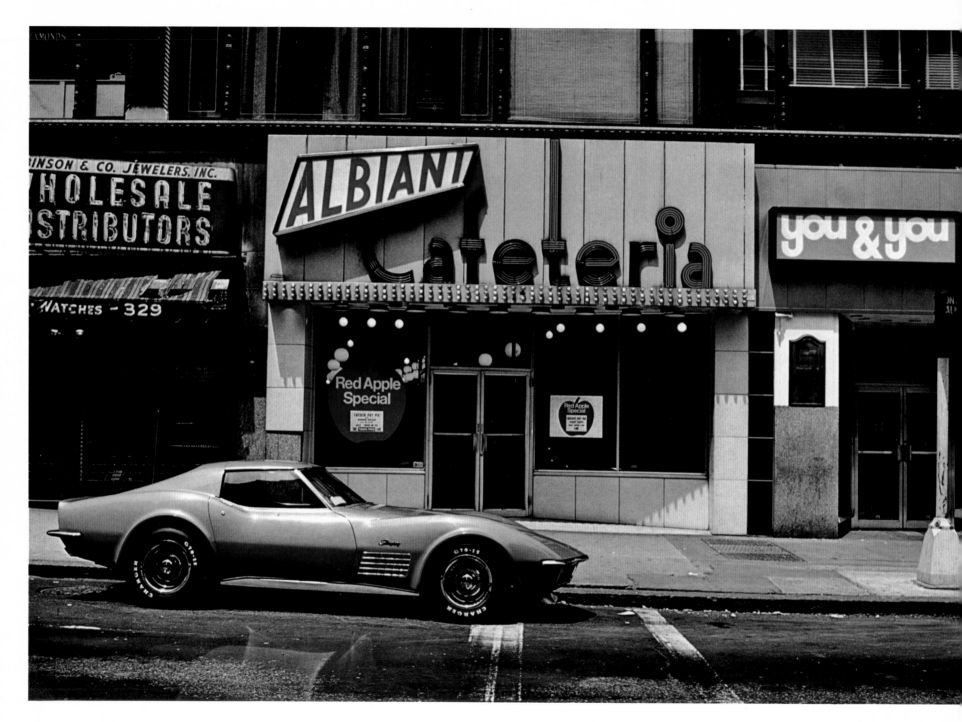

Washington Street

South End

View from Beacon Street

Detail, Christian Science Church

40

Detail, Quincy Market

South Boston

North End Playground

Chapel, North End

Light pole

Warehouses, South Boston

Remains of Railroad Station, Hyde Park

Daily Round

Stand outside Paul Revere's house, close your eyes, and look backward in time. Make the most of the only piece of seventeenth century Boston that is left, for it is a small gem among the parked cars, spilled oil, and windswept trash that give us a jolt of realism in the midst of our attempted nostalgia.

North Square was really a long, cobbled triangle, close to the waterfront, and was the center of town. It held a market, a guardhouse, and a busy town pump. There was the Mathers' Old North Meeting House, later razed by the British; Governor Hutchinson's mansion that was sacked by the mob at the time of the Stamp Act riots; and near them, Sir Harry Frankland's luxurious house, and the beautiful Old North Church, or Christ Church, where Paul arranged for the lanterns to be hung "two if by sea." The Revere house and the church are all that remain. At the turn of this century the house was restored to its present condition from an eyesore in the nineteenth. Built in 1676, in Paul's day it had three stories and seventeen windows. It may have had the third story when Paul bought it in 1770, or perhaps he added it to accommodate himself and his first wife Sara, his mother, an assortment of his children, some of his brothers and sisters, and probably apprentices as well. He fathered sixteen children, eight with each of his two wives, "Sary" and Rachel. He had a great love for his family, was always pleased to have another baby, and seems never to have considered them any kind of burden.

The frontage of the property was the same as it is now, but the land ran back to the Cockerel Church on Middle Street, and broadened out so considerably that Paul soon sold off a back lot, and still had room to build a horse barn afterwards. He owned a mare in 1773 but of course that was not the horse that carried him to immortality in posters, advertisements, and school books. He made a number of express rides on confidential business for the Provincial Congress, as he was energetic and reliable, and quite imperturbable under cross-questioning. But on the night of April 18, 1775, he had to leave Boston silently, and after crossing the Charles by rowboat, borrowed John Larkin's best horse, in Charlestown, for the ride that was to become the most famous of all, and he remembered the animal with gratitude for the remainder of his life.

Most of the North Square houses were lined up side by side on a level with the street, as there were no sidewalks, with ample room for farming behind. As the population increased a rash of back lot houses sprang up, reached by alleys, some of which were very narrow and unsavory. Nostalgia is all very well when viewed from the days of main drainage, but those privies and wells got all mixed up, and were responsible for many of the outbreaks of typhoid and "bloody flux." Fires, a constant threat of city life, were guaranteed by the close proximity of those little wooden houses, with their open fireplaces and combustible materials.

During the early years the streets had no numbers; hence the frequent changes in names, as that made it easier to find one's way. This was how trade signs came about. They were an advertisement that also formed a local guidepost, as they hung over the street so as to be seen from a distance. Ben Franklin's father used a blue bell, suspended by an iron rod over the southeast corner of Hanover and Union Streets.

The first generations of immigrants to this country had no problems adapting their standards of culture to the one they found here. What else would they do but behave and speak in the same way that they had at home? But as time progressed, the Atlantic became a wider barrier, culturally, as

*Expressway
expansion plates*

those who had been here for a generation or two would let the newcomers know that they were different, odd, and that they must adapt to American manners and speech. With each new arrival there would be the private conflict between wanting to retain the inner core of the homeland, and yet accept the mores of the adopted land, and how much of each to put into the children.

Paul Revere's father, Apollos Rivoire, had been just one of the 400,000 prosperous Huguenots who fled France during the one hundred years' purge of Protestants. They had gone to England, Switzerland, the Lowlands, and America; and the Faneuils and Bowdoins had already settled in Boston when Apollos arrived from the pleasant vineyard country near Bordeaux. As often happens in a war, he never saw his parents again. The French lad was in the charge of the ship's captain on that wintery voyage of 1715-16, and it had been arranged for him to work for John Coney, who had a shop in Anne Street, near Dock Square, and who was one of the finest goldsmiths of his day. (His work was stamped with a little rabbit.)

There were thirty-two goldsmiths at that time in Boston, though Bostonians wanted so many silver items for their churches, their persons, and their homes, that goldsmiths mostly worked in that metal instead, which aggravated the scarcity of hard money. Since there were no banks, when a household had a collection of various European coins it was taken to the local silversmith who turned it into porringers, cups, and tankards. (Traces of coins can be seen in some old silver flatware.) The shortage created in this way caused a need for paper money, and the first plates in America were engraved by Mr. Coney. He was a gentle, hard-working, church going man, who had three wives. With their assistance he produced twelve children, only five little girls surviving their

first year. Coney was not only to teach Apollos the skills of a goldsmith, but was responsible for turning him into a dependable citizen, and must have also helped him with the strange English tongue. Then, as now, foreigners had their names altered, willy nilly, into a more pronounceable form, and the name Apollos Rivoire suffered a translinguification into Paul Revere, "merely on account the Bumpkins could pronounce it easier."

The sedentary Boston apprentices wore leather breeches, baggily cut, so that they could be worn backside before, to even up the wear and tear. Thousands of other lads, in the cities of Europe, were learning everything from soap making to medicine. But if they did not show aptitude they could be returned to their parents to attempt a different trade.

By the time Paul Revere, Senior, was thirty, he had his own shop and a wife. He had married a neighbor, Deborah Hitchbourn, who came from a large and active family of artisans. She was thoroughly Yankee, and a strong vein of her independent, hardy, and courageous ancestors came out in her son Paul, whom she did not have until 1735, after she had been married six years. Granted, she had had a daughter first, but compared with other women of her time she was a long while getting on with the large family that was expected, in order to get the work done, and to have a fair percentage of them survive the hazards of childhood. In the next nine years Deborah caught up quite well and had seven more children, including a pair of twins, and losing only two babies. Young Paul was to live to be a very old man, as his life bridged over into the nineteenth century and the age of mechanization. He would roll the copper sheets for the dome of the State House, and for the *Constitution,* and make the plates for Robert Fulton's new-fangled steamships.

Paul's mother must have needed all her inherited strength and resourcefulness for running her busy and enlarging household. She would constantly be busy cooking, making cheeses, and preserves, and simple medicines, weaving cloth and making clothes, doing endless washing and baby tending, and looking after the domestic animals that were kept in the yard.

Household furnishings were simple in those days, with a few chests and cupboards, and a table with stools around it for meals. Many chairs of the time had rush bottoms, but cane was rare, though it had been introduced into English furnishings after Charles II married Catherine of Braganza in 1660. Easy chairs, copied from Dutch styles, were found in some homes. But the chief piece of furniture in most families was the parental bed, in which, on a lumpy mattress, life began and ended. Between these two extremes, on the cornhusks or the wool, were passed the loving, discussing, comforting, and suffering of the human animal. There are detailed descriptions of these beds in wills which go into considerable detail concerning stuffings, "pillars," and hangings. (A curtain lecture was a talking-to that one received behind the drawn bed-curtains.) There were trundle beds for the children, and there was even a colonial Murphy bed. Copied from the Dutch sleeping bench, it was hinged to a wall, usually in the kitchen, and let down at night onto supporting legs. When not in use it was hooked up to the wall, and had doors or curtains over it.

Privacy was an unknown luxury, and perhaps an undesired one, in every walk of life, both over here and in Europe. Families were huge, rooms were small. Every human relationship and function was a matter of curiosity and comment, on the part of family, neighbors, and clergyman. Children soon found out what death looked like, and were not long left in the dark as to how life began. This situation is found in all overpopulated areas of our present world, but the Japanese have skillfully circumvented the problem by being ultra polite and pretending not to hear or see what is not their business, thus providing the needed psychological space around each individual, for the preservation of sanity.

The older Revere's shop was attached to the house, with a furnace for melting the silver, and the sounds of his work would mingle with the domestic sounds of spinning wheel rattling, children crying and laughing, pot boiling, and chickens cackling; while outside, carts rumbled over the cobblestones and hawkers cried their wares in the street.

In 1743 the Reveres were renting a house on Dr. John Clark's wharf. Dr. Clark had lost forty ships in the French wars and so certainly had no extra silver to be made into trimmings, but in fact had been forced to sell his family mansion to Sir Harry Frankland, the Collector of the Port. Besides Sir Harry there were several other well-to-do families living in the North End who might need a christening mug, a pair of shoe buckles, a candlestick, or a spoon. One of these neighbors was Thomas Hutchinson, who was later to be governor; this charming, aristocratic man lived with his gardens, orchards, and coaches, in a pervasive air of what Samuel Johnson called, "the easy arrogance of wealth."

In contrast to the affluence enjoyed by the Reveres' Hutchinson neighbors there were many more citizens who scratched out a livelihood as best they could, by pilfering, pandering, and prostitution; in short, a typical European seaport existence. Differing incomes lived in close proximity in old Boston, and many of them knew each other, and came in frequent contact, as neighbors, as members of the same groups, and through their work.

When the younger Paul was a lad there were between fifteen and sixteen thousand people, most of them artisans whose services were basic to the continuing life of the town. In a modern town of that size a large number of the inhabitants get into their cars every day, and drive off to work in some place the rest of the town never sees, and there is little contact between the majority of the inhabitants, except at social gatherings, churches, or P.T.A. meetings.

The notion of parents having any say in the manner of their children's schooling would have been a quaint one to eighteenth century mothers and fathers. The young went off to study, and their parents heard nothing about it unless the child's behavior was bad. Childhood was brief, responsibilities were assumed early, and "spare the rod and spoil the child" was an accepted precept of the day. Learning was driven home in a variety of ways. Little children got taps on the head with a heavy thimble, and from there graduated to whipping, and other forms of torture that were conceived by ingenious and all-powerful teachers. There might be a large split twig placed on the child's nose to pinch until his eyes watered; or enforced balancing on a one-legged stool; or hitting with a blistering leather flapper attached to a stick. Even the young men at Harvard were publicly caned.

In the younger Paul Revere's time children went first to a dame school at a penny a week, where they also paid for their share of "firing" the building. The curriculum consisted of manners—heavy emphasis on this—the alphabet, and some reading. Spelling seems to have been a matter of individual choice, but penmanship was of the essence. Many Boston children had only a few years of this type of schooling.

There were also public schools, though in 1741 only 525 children attended. Many of the others were very likely kept at home to help with the work, or because they were sickly. The boys with a profession ahead went to Latin or grammar schools, up until the age of thirteen. To qualify for this kind of school the pupil had to be able to "read in the psalter." Classes were conducted the year round, except for a few holidays and special occasions such as a big fire, or the funeral of a local worthy. Reading was a noisy affair, with all the children chanting out loud, and was conducted on one floor, while penmanship, understandably, went on on another. Paper was too highly prized for children to waste, and carelessness—or any learning difficulty—was rewarded with a swift rap on the knuckles. (How different from now, when little children plow their way happily through reams of coloring paper.) If a boy was bright, and interested enough, he could continue his learning on his own. Paul was able to read chemical essays later on, and was said to be the only artisan in the country who could do so.

The attitude toward education varied in different parts of the country. A narrow-minded Englishman, writing from Virginia, in the seventeenth century said, "Thank God there are in Virginia no free schools nor printing, and I hope we shall not have, for learning hath brought disobedience and heresy into the world." Quakers thought the three R's were enough, and distinctly disapproved of any extended scholarship since it fostered undue pride and provoked idleness. Introduction of public schools among the German settlers was resisted by indignation meetings, and litigation. Tunkers (German Baptists) would have liked to destroy all books but religious ones, as schooling made boys lazy and dissatisfied on the farm, and gave them ideas that were inconvenient for their masters. School teachers in the middle and southern colonies were often redemptioners and exported convicts, and there was universal drunkenness among them. (One wonders how many modern teachers are driven to the bottle.) Scotland furnished the best, the most reliable, and the largest number of schoolmasters to the colonies.

In Massachusetts there was a better attitude, because a more educated group of people had settled the colony. Cotton Mather held the opinion that "the Youth in this country are verie Sharp and early Ripe in their Capacities." The first free Boston school was run by a man with the pleasing name of Philemon Pormont in 1634—the same year that Boston's first "ordinary" or tavern was licensed—and in time several million New England primers were printed, with their heavy stress on religion. Both boys and girls were sent to dame schools, but the girls were excluded from the booklearning. Boston's schools opened to girls in 1789, but up until then little girls were thoroughly grounded only in the arts they would need to become housewives. About the middle of the eighteenth century still only forty per cent of the female population could write, the others making their mark when required to.

Captain Marryat, an English naval officer, writer, and magazine editor, made an extended visit to this country in 1837. Like most of his countrymen he considered that the only nationality of true worth was his own, so when he encountered the same sentiment among Americans regarding theirs he regretfully had to consider them rather presumptuous, and concluded that this situation had arisen as a somewhat deplorable result of becoming a democracy. Concerning education he felt that the most important principle was *obedience*. He found American children woefully wayward, and was amazed at how society had been usurped by the young, but it is nice that he found parental control was the strongest in Massachusetts, and

reassuring that therefore (ergo) the education was probably superior. The captain felt that Americans were justly proud of their women, and did their best to educate them suitably, but not nearly enough time was allowed before marriage to give solidity to their knowledge. Marryat's own daughter was evidently brought up suitably, as she wrote 75 novels, several plays, her father's biography, and a number of works on spiritualism.

A couple of hundred years ago a woman had to be mistress of many skills in order to keep her household functioning smoothly. Female children learned their multiplication tables, and then went on to learn to cook and to brew, make preserves and medicines, spin, weave, sew, embroider, and knit, for their homes and for the shops. Fine work was well paid for and complicated stitches were managed by surprisingly young girls, who had their samplers to display, proudly, as proof of ability. Also there were lace-making, quilting, painting on velvet, paper cutting ("Papyrotamia"), and a great deal of intricate embroidery. Some stitches and designs have been traced back to Persian and Dutch ones; and as with Elizabethan words and phrases, some continued to be used over here but were no longer used in the mother country and have become extinct there. A few more fortunate little girls were also taught simple dance steps. In 1685 a dancing master, suitably named Francis Stepney, sought to set up "mixt Dances," but was hauled into court, and being unable to earn a living, ran away, with several attachments for debt out after him.

There was certainly no coddling of children, nor even of infants. Christening must take place shortly after birth, no matter what the weather. Ben Franklin, born on January 17, was whisked out in the cold three hours later to assure his being received into the church. One parson even practiced immersion, until his own child nearly died from being put into icy water. New babies were carried to church by the midwives, (with luck the mother was still resting), as they were important personages in the community. They boasted a very large number of deliveries in their professional lifetime, and if something went wrong there was probably no guilt feeling, as the Almighty just had not intended the baby, or perhaps the mother, to live. Infant mortality was horrifying by modern standards, but those that did survive were tough. As a woman approached middle-age she was more prone to produce stillborn or short-lived babies, and to die herself, in childbirth or soon after. But impending death was not kept from a sickly mother, so that she should have time to prepare for the "King of Terrors," and if her baby was not destined to reach maturity, that too must be accepted.

Soon after the baby's birth the midwife and other neighbor women were invited to a dinner at which they drank "groaning beer" and ate "groaning cake," "Rost Beef and minc'd Pyes," cheese, and tarts; boiled pork, fowls, turkey; and drank plenty of sack and claret. Women had not heard the theory that a lean mother makes a better nurse, but if there was any problem in the dairy department there was almost certainly another woman nearby with a baby, and she would help out as wet nurse. Failing that, there were pewter baby feeders, with a nozzle for the baby to suck cow's milk, and nobody gave a thought to pasteurization. After all even at Harvard the drinking vessels were scoured only once a week, and the plates but once in every two or three months!

Baby clothes were much embroidered. First chilly linen next to the skin, then sacks, and a cap all the year round until there was enough hair. For indispositions, something called "Daffy's Elixir"

was freely administered to babies. Worms, rickets, and fits were common ailments, and snails were the infallible remedy. (Well, amost infallible.) For snail water, or snail pottage, you "Take a peck of garden Shel Snails, wash them well in Small Beer, and put them in an oven till they have done making a Noise," (what kind of Noise?), "then take them out and wipe them well from the green froth that is upon them, and bruise them shels and all in a Stone Mortar, and take a Quart of Earthworms, scowre them with salt, slit them, and wash well with water from their filth, and in a stone Mortar beat them in pieces . . ." Had enough? And aren't we thankful that modern medicines are nicely encapsulated, keeping their ingredients a secret from our taste buds? But then were added flowers, herbs, ale, and beer, so perhaps after all it was a delicious "mixture as before," and such a concoction would cure a child of whatever ailed it. Snails applied externally were supposed to cure a rickety child, even one that went upon crutches. Also unguents to "anoynt" its breast; and drink for the "patient childe fasting"— snails with senna, rhubarb, and prunes cured worms and fits. Other horrible nostrums soothed the teething babe. This was all pretty trying for the children, but one cannot help thinking that it was rather hard on the snail population as well, and wondering which had the higher mortality rate.

Children grew up with death a frequent visitor to their own and playmates' families, and they were familiar with the Bible, especially the bits that warned of overdoing pleasure. But their short childhood was not entirely dreary. Youngsters had to be resourceful before the advent of television, and street games that date from several hundred years back are still played in the less privileged parts of the world—if privilege consists of "toy" guns, expensive bicycles, dolls that piddle and giggle, and all of them disappointingly susceptible to breakage. Jacks, marbles, and homemade dolls with a bit of cloth wrapped around them, left fewer dissatisfied children in their wake, but the contemporary child may be overwhelmed by our once-a-year gift compulsion, and often falls back on some friendly old toy he has had for years.

For sweetmeats the little New Englander had "glaz'd Almonds and rock-candy," and there were several kinds of fruit, though oranges were rare, and not wasted on children. There were gingerbread, Banbury "cacks" and "Meers cakes." (Meer was a famous Boston baker and confectioner.)

For reading, besides the Bible, there were other inspiring titles, such as "Spiritual Milk for Boston Babes in Either England. Drawn out of the Breasts of both Testaments for their Souls Nourishment." In 1787 relief arrived with "Peregrine Pickle Abridged," and "Vice in its Proper Shape," and for young men and ladies, "Fifteen Comforts of Matrimony," and "Laugh and be Fat."

An unlisted, but almost official, sin in the book of early Bostonians was that of being single—an attitude that has not entirely passed away. The unmarried, of either sex, were spied on, pressured, and jeered at by the community until most of them conformed. There was a practical reason behind this, since it was almost impossible to survive without a helpmeet. (For that matter, it was not too easy to survive with one, because of the succession of offspring, and all that they entailed.) But not many young women persisted in the state of maidenhood very long, as one was hopelessly on the shelf at twenty-five. "It is true an *old* (or superannuated) Maid in Boston is thought such a curse, as nothing can exceed it . . . about thirty years [old] (the age which they call a Thornback) . . ." The first matrimonial advertisement appeared in the *Boston Evening Post* of February 23, 1759. But caution had to be exercised over committing oneself, as many breach of promise acts were brought by men and women who had been jilted, or "shabbed." Once a promise had been made there was considerable freedom of action, as chaperonage was nonexistent until the end of the eighteenth century, when language became genteel and the frank approach to sex had vanished. Young people were not to enjoy such freedom again until Henry Ford came on the scene. When Paul Revere was courting his Sary, animal spirits were still allowed full rein, "When kisses and drams set the virgins aflame" . . . "while others, resolved to increase the uproar, Lay tussling the girls in wide heaps on the floor." And to think that generations of Americans have been raised on pictures of soberly dressed Puritans, with pure thoughts written all over their faces!

Curiously, the minister who advised the community could not solemnize weddings until the beginning of the eighteenth century. Before that, a magistrate, a captain, or any "man of dignity" would perform the ceremony. Many people had a succession of mates, but by reason of death, not incompatibility, as that would have been considered a luxury. Once widowed, no time was wasted in finding a replacement, as children needed care, and chores had to be done. One woman was even proposed to by number two at the graveside of number one. Perhaps she was known to be equable, or to have property, as marriage was a business contract. And for her part, a woman could not be indulged if she found it distasteful to use the same bed, pots, and pans as her predecessor. Duties, of all kinds, had to be done, but letters testify that there were many very happy marriages just the same.

Almost any old New England burying ground has instances of men being buried beside a series of wives. Often, however, the last wife survived her husband, and she was allowed to carry on his business, without that seven years' apprenticeship. In some cases, as with Paul Revere, Senior, there was a grown son to help. Paul was nineteen when the older Paul died, leaving no will, but "a good name and seven children." Paul was not permitted, by law, to take over his father's business until he was twenty-one, but he may have continued under his mother's name for a couple of years, until he went off to northern New York to fight in the French and Indian War. Many other businesses were run by capable female hands; one of Benjamin Franklin's sisters-in-law ran her late husband's soap-boiling business, and another was official printer for Rhode Island.

Boston's first newspaper had been attempted in 1690, but further publication was forbidden by the Governor's Council, as the paper contained " . . . sundry doubtful and uncertain Reports." The next effort was the *News-Letter*, in 1703, put out by a postmaster and printed on what is now Newbury Street. It was not a stimulating example. Most of the "news" items were taken from stale English papers; the local material was largely appeals for advertisements, and for backsliding subscribers to pay up for ads already printed. The *News-Letter's* apprentice was a natural-born gossip columnist before his time and channeled all the really interesting bits into his diary, because the boss did not consider them fit to print. So-and-so had left his considerable estate to one of his illegitimate offspring; or "Mr. John Hancock hath paid his addresses to Miss Sally Jackson for about ten years past, but lately sent her a Letter of dismission." A dead baby was found in a trunk, "which the Query of Inquest immediately sat on." This kind of titillation was denied the people, but in 1719 the *Gazette* appeared, and was more lively, as it contained articles by Sons of Liberty, under

assumed names, and it prospered. The *News-Letter* enviously commented, "I pity the readers of the new paper," and thereupon expired of neglect. The *New England Courant* was started by James Franklin in 1720 and by 1771 there were twenty-five newspapers altogether in America.

One of them was the very successful anti-Tory *Massachusetts Spy*, published by Isaiah Thomas, on the third floor of what is now the Union Oyster House. (Louis Philippe, future king of France, under the name of M. D'Orléans, earned some money by teaching French to a number of Boston merchants upstairs, as well.) Possessed of as much drive as Paul Revere, Thomas was to become the country's first great printer and publisher. Born in Boston, a Mason, and a Son of Liberty, he naturally knew Paul and they were friends all their lives. Paul did one of his views of Boston for Thomas' *Royal American Magazine,* and some more-or-less likenesses of John Hancock and Sam Adams, at least two of his prints being founded on Benjamin West's work. Copying other people was an unabashed practice of the time. In his silverwork Paul was superb; but knowing he was a poor draughtsman he often fell back on other people's ideas for his engravings.

Reading material was scanty, and since the only newspaper in town was to be found in the tavern, by the time everyone had perused it, it must have been thoroughly mangled. The ability to read was still not by any means universal, and one sign on a mantelpiece read: "Gentlemen learning to spell are requested to use last week's newsletter." More ambitious readers who desired books were obliged to send to England, but gradually the club rooms in taverns became a kind of lending library among their members.

Taverns were derived from an ancient institution (very likely thousands of years old) when they were almost entirely run by women. They were homes away from home, providing respite from the ordeals of travel, and their dreary descendants in the motel era are a travesty in which most things are either frozen or plastic.

The modern tour-guide bus driver is a reliable, but tame, descendant of the splendidly-dressed stage driver who whipped up his horses when a stop was just ahead, ignoring the additional jolts for the passengers. The stage was an important event in the community's life, and its arrival must be properly heralded with a suitable flourish. A responding agitation took place in the inn itself. Guests must be greeted, rested, and fed, but the coachman must first be brought his tankard of refreshment while still aloft on his seat. His dry throat must be attended to before those of the passengers. Their stiff muscles, new bruises, and empty stomachs will be assuaged shortly; then, once these creature comforts have been taken care of, news will be exchanged, and the stay-at-home inn help will get their second-hand glimpse of the romantic world outside.

By the nineteenth century, taverns had changed into places of a disorderly character, but in the seventeenth and eighteenth centuries they were still highly respectable, and there was a list of regulations to keep them that way. The price of meals and liquor was set by law. The publican was a respected and legally protected member of the community, who was fined for selling too much drink to any individual, but also fined if he refused to sell the amount permitted to be drunk in the place. Drinkers treated each other in turn, and then as now, efficient service was rewarded with a "tip" which was placed in a box labeled "To Insure Promptitude." A tally of each customer's intake was chalked up on the wall under "Pints & Quarts," so that it behooved him to mind his P's and Q's. In the fairly early days of the colony a ban on drinking had been imposed—and ignored, as it was considered a courtesy at weddings, church-raisings, and ordinations.

The average meal found in a Boston tavern was the best that the town could provide, with "no other formalities than such as good breeding required." The dinner hour was 2 p.m.: guests were summoned by a handbell rung in the street and an average of twenty people sat down to dinner. This was an age of repasts that would provide several meals today. There were no hors d'hoeuvres, or soups, but customers could expect solid helpings from a choice of venison, turtle, salmon, veal, beef, mutton, fowl, or ham, with vegetables and pudding. Carving was done at the table, and the guests could take what they preferred. A pint of Madeira, per person, washed all this down, and fruit, in the substantial shape of English tarts and cakes, filled any empty corners that might be left.

It was a practical matter of good business to care for the guests in the inn, to make them comfortable, and thus establish a good reputation. But also the concern was partly genuine, and not tainted with the phony hospitality of the modern turnpike "inn." The host aimed to make a visit as close as possible to the comforts of home, and if a traveler was ill, then he was nursed and looked after. When all was taken care of, and the guest must be on the road again, the bill was reasonable and did not smell of highway robbery.

The inn-keeper was a community leader, and a banker, pawnbroker, newsmonger, and friend to many of the guests. Sam and John Adams, William Penn, Andrew Jackson, and Abraham Lincoln, among others, were owners or operators of taverns. As all strangers were lodged under the same roof (and in a pinch, several in one bed), the constable kept an official eye on the lot of them. He

60

Lower Common

Public Garden

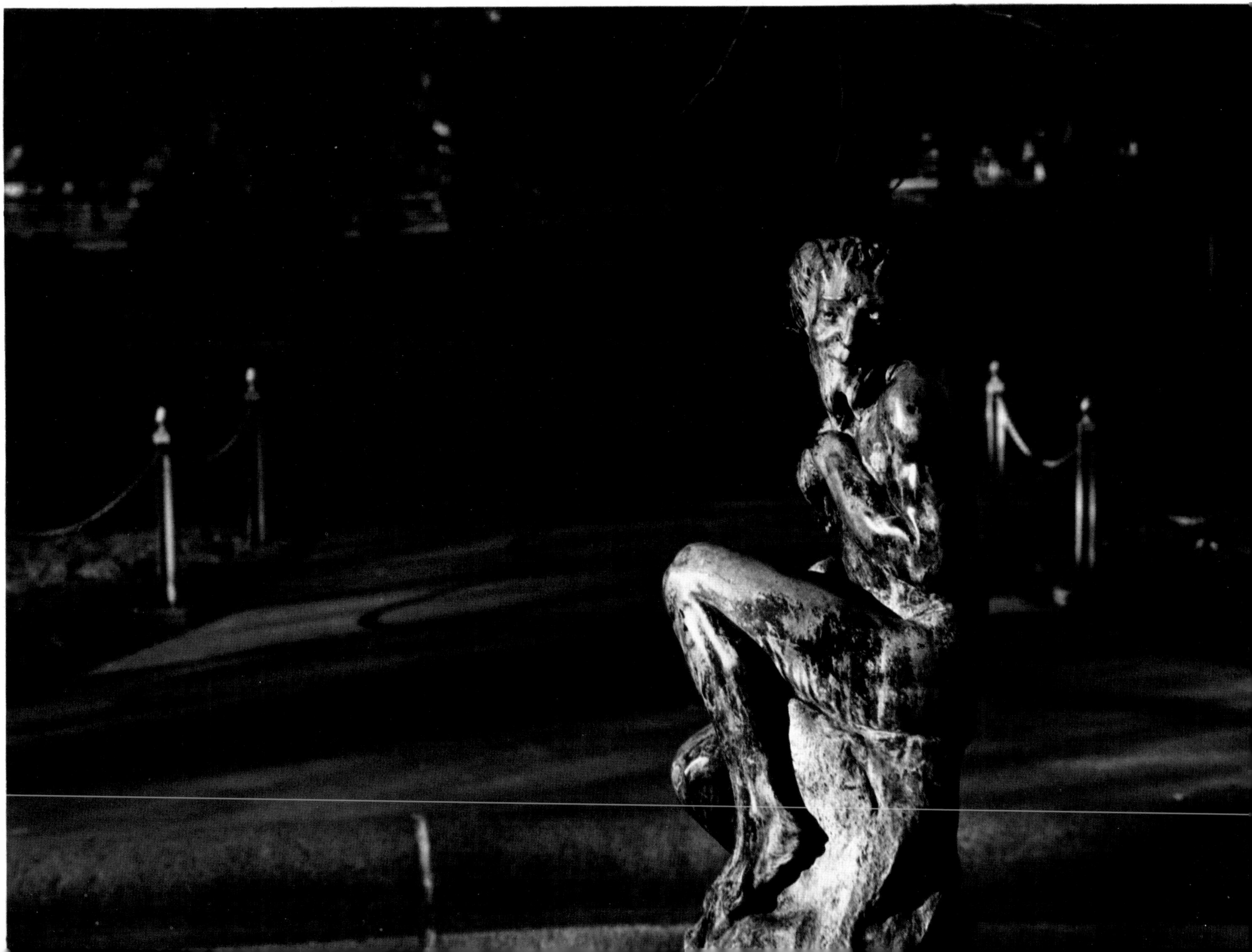

Figurehead,
Old State House

John Adams,
Faneuil Hall

Parking Garage

Men with hard hats

Fruit Seller, Haymarket

On the Common

was an authorized busybody, and recognized tale-bearer from house to house. Taverns were accepted necessities in the old country, and as each village was settled in the new colony, a strictly supervised tavern was licensed to take its place as an institution in the community. By 1675 every other house in Boston was an inn (or so Cotton Mather claimed, and surely he never lied.) Streets were named after them, and they quickly became known landmarks, as there were few public buildings. Travelers needed to know where their next stop was going to be, so the old almanacs measured distances between taverns rather than between towns; and arrival and departure times, with specific tavern names, were prominently advertised in town. Early inns were named after familiar ones at home: *Globe, Seven Stars, Red Lion, Lamb, George and Dragon,* and various-colored horses. The signs, which are now a disgraced form of art, were landmarks in themselves, familiar to everyone.

The only women to be seen in taverns were travelers, aside from those who worked on the premises, for although numerous men of the town took their daily dinners at the local tavern, their womenkind stayed at home, or visited each other's houses. Taverns became established as men's clubs, where political and business gossip were exchanged. Among the upper class, women did go to private dinners and dances, though only the young danced, as middle-age had descended by one's thirties; but even fairly recently in this group it was customary for the ladies to retire after dinner to the (with)drawing-room to let their men smoke, drink port, and talk "male" talk for a while. In a previous era when men proved their stamina by drinking each other under the table, the drawingroom was a blessed haven for the women.

The colonists in the second half of the eighteenth century managed to put away unbelievable quantities of intoxicating fluids. Rum was taken neat or in a punch. John Hancock kept a jug of it on his sideboard, round the clock, and his daily intake began with a morning tankard of hot rum punch. Wine was also accounted for by the gallon at every dinner. And the toasts! Healths were drunk to every conceivable rank and grade of authority, and to every imaginable interest. Besides wine there were other gradual aids to the horizontal position: flip was ale, beer, and cider, spiced, sweetened, and heated with a hot iron; and negus was a brew made of wine, water, lemon juice, sugar, and nutmeg. This last was not as innocuous as it sounds, and had a way of creeping up on the unwary. It is anyone's guess how much history has come under the influence—not only of liquor, but of the hangover as well.

Taverns were also the place to smoke. Long before moderns discovered the horrible effects of tobacco, the founding fathers looked upon it as a far more harmful indulgence than intoxicating liquor. Smoking was "sinful, hurtful, and degrading," and most New England settlements forbade the planting of tobacco. Smoking of the noisome weed must be done in the most secluded fashion—in other words, isolate the addicts!—and the smoking room was initiated in taverns so that the rest of the house and the guests need not be distressed by the smoke. There was even a fine if a smoker puffed in any other part of the tavern. (Two traveling Dutchmen, when visiting part of Harvard, were so overcome upon entering that they were certain it must be a tavern's smoking room.)

This courtesy to non-smokers lasted many years. Trains had special compartments for smoking; and in the Victorian age gentlemen went outside the house to smoke, to avoid upsetting the sensibilities of their womenfolk, or they smoked in the downstairs lavatory, or "cloakroom" which was the province of the men of the house. In 1917 there were still men living who had been asked to plead guilty or not guilty, to smoking in Boston's streets. Policemen suggested that offenders show respect (lip service?) to an extinct statute by tossing their cigars into the gutter. Now non-smokers, after fifty years of being non-people, are once again finding a response to their complaints, and there are refuges for them in many public places.

With transportation so difficult, and towns so sparse, the tavern became the social center, and each had its own flavor, as the location determined what type frequented it. Among Boston's dozens of taverns, *The Salutation* became the meeting-place of shipwrights and caulkers—hence "caucus"—and Sam Adams, taking advantage of their clannishness, molded them into a group to suit the Whigs. *The Crown Coffee House,* on Long Wharf, was a favorite haunt of the young bucks of the town, and of visiting seamen, who regaled their audiences with lurid tales of buccaneering. Many taverns had historical events hatched in them. *The Green Dragon* was headquarters of the Saint Andrew's Lodge of Masons, and a stopping-place for racing enthusiasts on the way to their favorite raceground at (now) Revere Beach, as well. In 1740 a balloon was sent up from the *Dragon,* and thirty-three years later plans were laid for another kind of balloon to go up—the Boston Tea Party.

At *The British Coffee House,* in 1750, there had been an attempt at staging a play, but there was such a struggle to get in, that a riot ensued: Boston was that starved for theatrical entertainment. A few years earlier efforts at theater had been made, and squelched, but this later one caused a law to be passed prohibiting ". . . theatrical entertainments . . ." as they " . . . greatly increase impiety." If it

was anything like the average Restoration play, the ribald phrases would have fallen on very receptive ears. But gradually ways were found to get round the law, as usual, and plays were performed under the guise of "readings." Legitimate theaters opened in the last decade of the eighteenth century, concentrating on English ballad-operas; but that was too late for the occupying British before the Revolution. A bored young officer complained to his diary that he had never seen a town with so many whores; but there was no theater, and nothing else to do. There were hundreds of these women in wooden shacks by the waterfront and on Mount Vernon ("Whoredom"). Evidently the young man was not in the mood for music, or he might have found pleasant company in one of the taverns, as landlords kept musical instruments on hand for the benefit of the patrons, who could keep warm by playing and singing, as well as by drinking hot toddy.

In our mechanical age it is hard for the average person-in-the-street to imagine what fun it was to provide one's own entertainment by filling in with a voice part or an instrument. We have become thoroughly spoiled by hearing the world's best performers reproduced with better-than-likely quality; and yet there is an impersonal feel to it, and though lacking the distractions of a live performance, it also lacks some of the individual personality of the artists. Public concerts, with admission price, did not occur even in London until the late seventeenth century, and were held—where else —in taverns. The first authentic record of a public concert in any English-speaking colony was December 30, 1731, in Boston. Peter Faneuil's Hall was not built until 1741, and only just was built at all, as those favoring it won by only seven votes. That first concert was held in Mr. Pelham's "great Room" and "N.B. There will be no admittance after

Six"! There were very likely baby-sitter and traffic delays then as now, but audiences were to consider the performers, and accept disciplinary treatment by the management.

Toward the end of the seventeenth century books of instruction and ruled paper came from England, along with larger musical instruments. The organist of King's Chapel advertised these, and "also repair of same." And *he* ran a dancing school as well. Early in the 1730's the first noted European musician to visit Boston was Karl Theodore Pachelbel, and after the Revolution there was a beneficial influx of scores of foreign musicians, who were both composers and performers.

America's first home-grown composer was William Billings, a tanner by trade, and he published "The New England Psalm Singer" in 1770, the same year that Beethoven was born. Paul Revere made the engravings for it, and also the frontispiece of some men in full dress and powdered wigs, seated around a table, singing. Blind in one eye, with a withered arm, legs of different lengths, a loud, rasping voice, and slovenly appearance, he was a perfect example of nature choosing to put her talents in an unlikely vessel. He had no musical knowledge, but great enthusiasm, and became so engrossed in making melody, that he gave up his business and had difficulty supporting his wife and six children. He lies in an unmarked grave in the small burial ground on the Common. There was no money for a headstone. In 1764 Paul Revere had published a collection of Psalm tunes, in conjunction with Josiah Flagg, the jeweller, and they were advertised in the *Boston Gazette*. Flagg also formed and trained a military band, and often organized concerts. In 1771 he promoted one in which the music of Bach and Händel was performed.

Peter Pelham, the owner of the great room, had arrived from England a few years before that first concert, and was engraver, portrait painter, teacher of dancing, writing, reading, painting on glass, and all sorts of needlework. He taught "from Candle-light 'till nine in the Evening, as usual, for the benefit of those employ'd in Business all the Day." (Possibly the first colonial night school.) In 1748 he married the widow Copley, who ran her late husband's tobacco shop on Long Wharf, and thus he became the stepfather of ten-year-old John Singleton Copley. After three years Peter died, and John went to work in Peter's studio with its equipment for mezzotints and painting. John had a very close relationship with his halfbrother, Henry Pelham, who was twelve years younger, and painted him in his teens as "Boy with a Squirrel." Henry was to become a very fine miniaturist, and it was he who was so enraged with Paul Revere for plagiarizing his engravings of the Boston Massacre.

When the first New England settlers came over, an interest in painting had to come, of necessity, after the essentials of life. These immigrants had been accustomed to having skilled craftsmanship among their possessions in England, but over there art was still ecclesiastical, or a royal luxury, at the time of the exodus to America. It was not until the mid-eighteenth century that there was enough prosperity to keep a portrait painter alive in the colonies. The early limners, who traveled with completed portraits, except for the face, had branched out from sign or coach painting, as the demand for "likenesses" began to take hold. Then John Smibert and Robert Feke became known and established in New England, and Copley a bit later on.

Smibert was to have taught art and architecture in Bermuda, in Dean Berkeley's proposed college for the Christian civilization of the American Indian, in 1728, but the rather dubious project folded, due to lack of funds. Smibert came to Boston, where he was the most skillful painter yet to have worked in the town, or anywhere in the colonies. Born in Edinburgh, he had traveled widely in Europe, collecting copies of old masters, casts of sculpture, and prints, all of which he must have meant to use in Bermuda. In Boston he created a sensation by exhibiting them, with his own paintings, in his studio in what was to become Scollay Square. This, with his adjacent shop, was the first art center in America, (Scollay Square, like the Cheshire Cat, faded away again, and was replaced by Government Center.) To begin with, Smibert was unrivaled, but as his health and sight began to fail, in the seventeen forties, the first generation of native-born painters started to compete with him: Robert Feke, John Greenwood, Joseph Badger, and Smibert's talented son, Nathaniel.

As there was a dearth of architects in the eighteenth century, cultivated amateurs were able to show their creativity. Smibert did the original plans for Faneuil Hall, which were later enlarged and changed by Bulfinch. Peter Harrison, a contemporary of Smibert, though having no professional training, became the most distinguished architect of the colonial era, and designed King's Chapel.

Nathaniel Smibert died at twenty-three, leaving young Copley master in an artistically active town. He worked artisan's hours, often as much as sixteen at a stretch, and expected his sitters to lump it somehow, and to avoid looking cramped, bored, or merely stuffed. There were often fifteen or sixteen sittings for a portrait, but as commissions poured in, there were evidently plenty of patrons to endure his frenzy of work. He was annoyed that most people considered him no more than a craftsman, like "a Carpenter, tailor or shew maker, not as one of the most noble Arts in the World." The majority of them wanted their likeness because of the usual human reasons of vanity, for posterity, or so that they could send their portraits to relatives in Britain (though a miniature was more convenient for this). A portrait was also a stand-in for a loved one, and therefore much more desirable than a landscape or historic subject. Many pairs of portraits were done to celebrate a marriage or anniversary. Much of Copley's work was done in exchange for merchandise, and it is highly probable that he did Paul Revere on this basis, as it is known that Paul applied silver and gold leaf to frames that he bought from other craftsmen. The portrait is of Revere at about thirty-five, in working clothes, with his own hair. A finished teapot rests on a hammering pillow, ready for decoration. One hand supports Paul's head—"the source of his inspiration"—and the other the finished piece of work. His jaw is firm and his look direct. It is a good-natured face, but not one that would put up with any insolence.

Boston was a town where elegant clothes were seen every day of the week, and the males of the species were every bit as dazzling as the females—though pity the man who had to reveal a pair of spindly legs in those demanding silken hose. Boston was not a true democratic melting-pot like Philadelphia, and later, when John Hancock was the first Federal Governor, he became known as an ostentatious figure who traveled with six horses and four servants. Most of Copley's work was done for comfortably-off merchants, and the ladies who wore those bare-chested dresses were borne about the streets of the town in carriages or in sedan chairs, which were usually carried by Chinese bearers. Copley used to pile on bizarre clothes to keep himself warm in cold weather, but his female sitters must have been half frozen in their satins and laces, unless someone kept a roaring fire going for them.

Or, if the political wind from England was fair, they probably drank tea to keep their toes warm during a rest from posing. But as 1773 drew nearer the importation of tea and other luxuries for consumption by the well-to-do became less tactful, as far as the Boston populace was concerned. Ladies proved their allegiance to the cause of justice from the mother country by abstaining from tea, and spread the word that the herb was a pernicious destroyer of the texture of the human stomach, as well as a cause of relaxation, dejection, and hysteria. Tea was a touchy subject with Copley. He had a natural disinclination for becoming embroiled in politics and painted Whigs and Tories alike, but his father-in-law, Richard Clarke, was nephew of Governor Hutchinson, and also the major consignee of the taxed tea. When the mob smashed Clarke's windows in November, 1773, Copley attempted to mediate between the radical leaders and his merchant in-laws, without success. Then the Boston Tea Party took place on December 16, but it was not the kind of social event that one brags about, and everyone who attended was naturally reticent afterwards, fearing lawsuits by the East India Company. The *Massachusetts Gazette* of December 23, 1773, related in semi-Biblical language that the tide floated the broken chests, and the tea, "insomuch that the surface of the water was filled therewith." The tea drifted as far as Dorchester Neck, and the next morning a windrow of the stuff extended from the wharves to Castle Island, which at that time was well out to sea. If a fourth ship had not been wrecked on Cape Cod there would have been even more. (Also in this fourth tea ship were three hundred latest model white globe lamps for Boston's streets. John Hancock master-minded this project and Paul Revere was also on the committee.

Providentially, the lamps survived the wreck.)

Copley's middle-of-the-road attitude protected his art, and he had become well-to-do. After a childhood spent on Long Wharf he ascended, residence by residence, to a house on Beacon Hill, near the Hancock estate, owning twenty acres, three houses, a barn, and an orchard, and called his rural haven Mount Pleasant. But he had always hankered to go to England, and his patronage was dropping off by 1773 because of the political upheavals—his sitters had more urgent things to do with their time and money. Never anticipating armed conflict, he went over in 1774, leaving his family to follow him, and expecting, as so many loyal exiles did, to return to America later on. Having arrived where he wanted to be, he changed his style to emulate the English painters and had no trouble getting commissions, some of them from Americans visiting London; but he yearned to be known as a historical painter, and his huge canvas "The Death of Lord Chatham" established him in this category. America had lost a great leader in portraiture, as he became slick in England, and lost the powers of selection and the honesty of his American period. He never did come back home.

Paul Revere had taught himself engraving to supplement his income, and became very skillful, but in 1768 he also learned the trade of dentistry. Travelers from Europe often mentioned the deplorable condition of New Englanders' teeth, and one of them commented that the women were "pitifully Toothshaken." Were the men's teeth better, due to less sweet eating, or was a male observer more concerned over the appearance of girls? For this condition began at 18 or 20 and was attributed by one visitor to hot bread and too much tea. A Swedish scientist, Peter Kalm, had written twenty years earlier that the sad plight of young women's teeth might be due to the air, and the frequent sudden changes in the New England climate, "for the end of a hot day often turns out piercing cold and vice versa." (Yes indeed.) And yet he observed that Indians did not shed their teeth. Perhaps the trouble lay with the great quantities of fruit and sweetmeats; but he had known many people who never ate any fruit, and still had hardly a tooth left. He decided to blame it all on tea; but then he met a number of young women born in Europe who had lost most of their teeth when they came to America, before they ever began to drink tea. Kalm continued to theorize, but did not convince even himself.

Revere started cautiously with dentistry, advertising only to clean teeth and replace "foreteeth." He learned these arts from an English Surgeon-Dentist named John Baker, who was in Boston for many months, staying at the *Cromwell's Head*. (This was the tavern where the sign hung so low that passers-by either had to duck, and in doing so pay homage to the Lord Protector, or cross the street and snub him.) After Mr. Baker went back to England, Revere advertised in the Boston Gazette of September 19, 1768 "WHEREAS many Persons are so unfortunate as to lose their Fore-Teeth . . . they may have them replaced with artificial ones, that looks as well as Natural, & answeres the End of Speaking to all Intents . . ."

Probably the dental job that was most important to Paul was the one he did for his longtime friend, Dr. Joseph Warren. Paul was never an eloquent speaker, but Warren was, and for that alone he would need respectable teeth. Paul was dark and sturdy. Warren was fair and blue-eyed, and "irritable," meaning lively and full of sensibility. He was kind, enthusiastic, intelligent, and had a fine appearance, and his patients particularly liked the fact that his hands were clean! This was a rare quality, even in doctors, and their neglect of this nicety was one of the ways in which they spread disease so effectively, especially childbed fever. Paul wired in two teeth for his friend, and it must have been one of the saddest days of his life when, after Bunker Hill, he identified Warren's body by the teeth. Warren had been shot in the face.

This country knew even less than England and France about teeth, and still hoped to cure toothache by carrying a dead man's tooth in a pocket, or by stuffing the sore place with mastick. There was no preventive dentistry until the last half of the nineteenth century when Greene Vardiman Black created it as a new science, based on clinical observation, combined with his vast knowledge of physics, chemistry, anatomy, histology, physiology, bacteriology, and pathology. If you lived in the wrong century the family doctor did what he could with wrenches, "keydraughts," and "neat hawksbills." If you didn't have a doctor, then a barber, or even the local blacksmith could do the job for you—or on you. A muscular friend would help hold you down, while the tooth, the instrument, or even the jaw got broken in the process. Our diarist friend Judge Sewall recorded that he did not have the "Resolution to go thro' the Operation." (And now we even have the luxury of analgesic gases!) If the torture was reasonably successful, the patients, or victims, were left with unsightly gaps, or were mumble-mouthed, or hollowed-cheeked, which accounted for the prevalent look of old age before its time. Paul's second wife, his "dear girl" Rachel was painted at sixty-eight by Gilbert Stuart, and has a sweet old lady's smile, with tucked-in cheeks; Paul, painted at the same time, and ten years older, evidently still had his teeth.

Isaac Greenwood, one of Revere's neighbors on Clark's Wharf, was a mathematical instrument-maker and ivory-turner, who made "billiard balls, flutes, handles for coffee pots, warming pans, and walking sticks. Also wooden legs and umbrillos." He may have made the teeth for Paul's patients, and after the Revolution, when Paul gave up dentistry, Greenwood fixed "natural teeth on plates of gold or silver with gold springs if wanted," and "they do give a youthful air." (The Etruscans had made removable bridges long before Greenwood.) At this time teeth were filled with gold, though not yet drilled, and called plugged, or with lead, and called plumbed. (Well, we still have lead in some of our paints, and gasoline, don't we?) Of Greenwood's four sons who took up dentistry, it was John who went to France to study the latest methods, and who invented the foot-power drill, the use of porcelain in making false teeth, and the implanting of human teeth, which were supplied by indigents, rather as blood came to be supplied by drug addicts in our time. John Greenwood was the man who made the famous hinged teeth for Washington, as well as other sets for him. Poor George became quite dependent on his dentist.

Elephant tusks discolored too quickly, so Paul used "teeth and tusks of the hyppotomus or sea horse," or animal teeth, au naturel, whose unhuman shape made them difficult to fit satisfactorily; and there must have been some startling smiles. Occasionally a tooth or two could be wired to neighboring teeth, or fastened in with silk, as the Egyptians had done. (They also attempted implantation of human teeth, culled from an inexhaustible supply of slaves.) As he improved, Paul advertised that he could fix teeth as well as any Surgeon-Dentist who ever came from London, and that they could actually be used for speaking and eating (what a relief), and that he would wait on any gent. or lady at their lodgings. He also advertised dentifrice, and it seems that almost any abrasive would

do. Contemporary recipes suggested ground-up pieces of crockery, cuttle-bone, coral, brown sugar candy, saltpeter, gunpowder, and white bread crumbs. And formulae for cleaning and whitening; "sopes," blanches, and tooth rakes; and probably tongue scrapers as well.

But Paul was not interested enough, or perhaps inventive enough, to add to the current knowledge of the craft, and gave it up after a few years. However, Josiah Flagg, with whom Paul had rung bells in their youth, and later published music, had a son who made dentistry his life work. As a lad he had "utterly repudiated books" (a sure recipe for success in the world of free enterprise), but somehow his interest was caught, and he became a devoted student of medicine and surgery. He devised a traction system for broken bones, and practiced dentistry in Boston, designing the first set of forceps for human teeth. He also invented "mineral" teeth, which were not corruptible.

However, the human body was always subject to deterioration. The poor and indigent had been given into the care of reliable older women in the seventeenth century, who were paid for their efforts by the town. But no sympathy was wasted on these unfortunates, as their condition was the will of God, especially if the person was not a church member. An insane person's family was supposed to get together to pay for their relative, but if not, then the town became responsible for him too. In the eighteenth century many of them were boarded in the country (one patient was a son-in-law of Paul Revere), where they were well cared for, unless they were put in an almshouse, where they often were beaten and died of neglect. In Europe the insane were frequently treated in an unspeakable manner, or left entirely alone. But gradually a more humane and scientific outlook developed, as the eighteenth century approached.

Thomas Hancock, among others who were trying to improve social evils, left £1,000 in 1764 toward the care of Boston's lunatics, and the kindly Paul Revere considered his son-in-law to be mentally ill, and not a malingerer.

And then, besides all the usual diseases, there were intermittent outbreaks of smallpox, with bouts counting as epidemics at longer intervals. In 1721 there was one of these, and half the population of Boston was afflicted, with one out of six of them dying. Hundreds of survivors, from rich to poor, carried pitted, disfigured faces in those days; one of them was George Washington, who was observed to have a scarred face when he visited Boston as a young man, and stayed at the *Cromwell's Head.* Inoculation, as practiced in the Orient and Near East, was described in a pamphlet sent from England during the 1721 epidemic. When Zabdiel Boylston inoculated his own son, rage and fear spread in waves through the people, and the doctor was mobbed in the street. Every doctor in Boston, except Boylston, opposed inoculation, and every clergyman was in favor of it.

In the 1763 outbreak pesthouses were instituted. These were empty houses outside the town and were greatly feared as being a place to die; even calling them hospitals did nothing to convince people of their safety. Watchmen who had already had smallpox kept guard in the streets, with a flag outside each house where there was a case. The law required that a report be made to the selectmen when a case appeared in a family, and in February of that year Paul Revere reported that one of his children had the dreaded disease. But he would not let his "lamb" be taken to the pesthouse. A flag was hung outside the Revere home, with a Mr. Murphy as watchman, and they had to be self-sufficient for a month, as Paul's books show there were no orders taken for silverwork during that time. None of the children died, but Sary was expecting once more and the baby was born before the quarantine was up.

Smallpox begins with a fever, but a rash comes out on the third day, usually starting on the face. People clung to the faint hope that it might only be another of the spotted miseries, but then came the sharp rise in temperature and the characteristic pustules erupted with their accompanying odor. The outbreak of the 1760's was at first confined to the North End, but by March it was all through the town, and many people fled to the country. Selectmen took their courage in both hands, many of them remembering the hysteria of forty years earlier, and decided to allow inoculation. (There was no cowpox vaccination until the end of the century.) A needle, bearing a little "venom" from "the best sort of smallpox" was used to make a small wound, and the resulting mild case conferred immunity on the sufferer. The inoculation was free, and many outsiders from nearby towns "obtruded themselves" and were treated as Bostonians. By May the nineteen doctors were thanked for carrying out their difficult task, and by the end of June everything was under control: 4977 people had been inoculated, 46 of them had died; 699 had contracted it in the normal way, and of these 124 had died. Among the pioneering doctors were Benjamin Church, and Joseph Warren, who inoculated John Adams and began a close relationship with him. The seeds of smallpox- and tyranny-prevention were being disseminated together.

Everybody knows the story of Paul Revere's ride. Or they think they do; but it is best not to rely too heavily on Longfellow as he had not read Paul's own account, although it had been published. In the mid-eighteen hundreds America was ready to lap up romantic tales of her folk heroes, and enthused over Longfellow's version that had Paul watching for the signal on the wrong side of the river and as the solitary rider on that night, and claimed that he went as far as Concord. But perhaps there is some poetic justice in the fact that when the centennial of the Battle of Lexington was held, twelve years after Longfellow's poem was published, the poor poet missed all the to-do because it was a "Bad day for me; neuralgia raging," and his daughters saw it all without him. One nice point that might have appealed to Longfellow enough to include it in the tale was that Revere left his house that night without his spurs; but fortunately his dog trotted after him, and when Paul realized that the spurs were missing, he tied a note to Rachel onto the dog's collar, and sent him home. In a short while back came the dog, with the spurs, and Paul and his two companions went on their way. All we know about the helpful dog is that it cannot have been a large one. Forty-seven years earlier, butchers had become so infuriated by dogs worrying their animals, both before slaughter and afterwards, that the town had ruled that dogs must not be more than ten inches tall. But Sam Adams owned a huge Newfoundland, named Queque, who was regularly taunted by British soldiers, and who soon formed the habit of attacking a redcoat on sight. Such a commendable dog was naturally exempt from the law.

If Longfellow missed the battle's centennial, Revere missed the real thing, because he was rescuing John Hancock's trunk from the Buckman Tavern, near the Green. The trunk was full of state papers that Hancock needed to take with him to Philadelphia. Imagine Paul, and John Lowell, Hancock's secretary, trying to be unobtrusive, staggering along with a large, metal-bound, nail-studded trunk, while the fatal shot was fired. If Paul saw which side it came from, he never told. He seems not to have had the urge to fling himself into battle, but very sensibly saved himself for other, more lasting, exploits. He had seen enough grim soldiering in his youth.

He did do a few years' duty at Castle Island, and there were some military expeditions that he took part in. He got home often enough to make some silver—and his son Joseph Warren was born in 1777, the son who would live to head one of America's largest industries, Revere Copper, and to die at the age of ninety-one. Also that year the country had its first Fourth of July celebration, and Paul was ordered to fly flags and fire guns for the country's first birthday.

The war dragged on, the way wars do, and when it was over there was a great deal of building up to be done. The remaining Continental army was disbanded and the men returned home to find no jobs, as so often happens to service men, in whom nobody is much interested when their fighting is done.

There were sobering changes in Boston: earthworks on Copp's Hill, at the Neck, and on the Common; trees, including the Liberty Tree, had been cut down by the British for fuel; food was extremely scarce; disease rampaged. Places of worship had been razed or used for pigs or horses, and nearly every house belonging to the ordinary mortals had been pillaged. The homes of the upper crust, however, had been left untouched, to provide quarters for the officers. Even the home of the ultra-patriotic John Hancock was not damaged, though it had been used as a hospital. General Gage, Lord Howe, Sir Harry Clinton, and Earl Percy were quartered there at various times, and were evidently not only officers, but also gentlemen. En masse, the occupying British were mostly barbarians, but taken a few at a time, not bad fellows at all. After the war Hancock House was again the scene of dinners, balls, and official ceremonies. With the elegant clothes, colorful uniforms, and august personages that were guests, the house might well have vied in splendor with the prewar flavor that had prevailed at Province House, the Royal Governor's mansion—the royal flavor that America had been so eager to cast off. The postwar gorgeousness was acceptable, however, as long as it was not imposed from without.

Now there was a different revolution under way; the class system was turned topsy turvy, which was nice for the "lower orders," but took some accommodating by the upper ones, although Boston had never been as class conscious as England. The former mother country sent over a flood of manufactured goods, hoping to revive the old trading cameraderie, and found a co-operative, though unthinking, market among the peace-happy people of Boston. The *nouveaux riches* were more than willing to dress to the nines in silks and perfumes, but all the furbelows had to be imported, for which they could only offer ashes, tar, and codfish. How familiar it all would have sounded to Thomas Hancock.

Paul Revere's ledgers record new names, but his calm temperament was not much upset by the changeover, as long as he could support his family. Although many Boston merchants smuggled in English goods before the Treaty of Paris, Revere did not, but was ready to bring them in as soon as he legally could. Two weeks after the signing of the Treaty on September 3, 1783, a ship left London with 500 pounds of goods for Paul to sell in Boston. The agents were his old prewar friends who had emigrated, but there were no hard feelings between them. He paid off his debt to at least one of them by making, and sending over, spoons in lieu of money.

When his goods arrived he opened up a shop opposite the Liberty Pole that had replaced the Liberty Tree, in what is now the heart of the honky-tonk "Combat Zone." We can see from Paul's lists what Boston most lacked. There were hardware, various weights and types of cloth, clothing, toupées, sandpaper, blotting paper, foolscap, wallpaper, sealing wax, inkhorns, playing cards, and "messanger cards." Also pencils, spectacles, and "visuals," fishing lines, pumice stones, and large amounts of plated silver. He paid for these in regular currency, in Spanish milled dollars, or by ingots he made himself from sweepings from his workshop, or even from melted gold lace. When he moved the site of his shop again to 50 Cornhill, the old shop became a bookshop under Ebenezer Larkin, nephew of the man who had lent his willing, reliable horse to Paul for the ride to Lexington.

By now the world had opened up considerably to Boston. Her ships were going to China, Java, and India. The China trade ships, rounding Cape Horn, picked up otter skins from the northwest coast Indians and took them across to China, bringing back a whole new epoch in design and viewpoint. New exotic aromas were now smelled in the town, little monkeys were stylish as pets, and new materials were available for personal adornment. And also there was money: lots of money, in some cases, and Paul once more had wealthy patrons for whom to create his silverwork. Elias Hasket Derby of Salem was one of his best customers. It was Derby's *Grand Turk* that made the initial round trip to Canton, bringing back the first Chinese porcelain to come directly to Boston. Paul was delighted with its design, and it became a new influence on his work. Some of the *Turk's* magnificent woodwork was done by the Skillin brothers, who made an eleven-foot-tall *Turk*, as well as brackets, trail boards, catfaces, trusses, and heavily carved festoons. McIntyre, the famous Salem architect and carver, finished her cabins, and Robert Gowans, painter of sleighs and coaches, added ornamentation.

Also the new country was getting a navy together, and John Skillin carved the heads for six new frigates, one of them the *Constitution*. Paul made the bell for her, but it was not his first bell. That one had been for his own church, and sounded "panny, harsh and shrill." However, he was not a man to make the same mistake twice, and from the many letters about his bells we learn that he was very proud that there had never been a breakage or a complaint of the sound. Sometimes it was he that had cause for complaint, as several of his so carefully made bells were hung incorrectly by the buyer, causing strain on them, so they could not be rung correctly. An estimate was made in 1911 that he and Joseph Warren Revere must have made about four hundred bells. The largest and most famous one is still hanging in the brooding stone tower of King's Chapel, and it was cast in 1816 at Paul's Canton foundry, with wealthy vestrymen throwing silver into the mix to ensure the beauty of its sound. (That was Canton, Massachusetts, which had been named because of its supposed antipodal location to the Chinese Canton). Paul considered it "The sweetest bell we ever made."

George Washington died at the end of 1799, and in January, 1800, Boston's Masons put on a truly splendid memorial procession. The Unitarian minister from Salem preached the sermon, and, exhausted after the seven hours of funerary excesses, accepted Revere's invitation to supper. Another guest was Mason Isaiah Thomas, who had progressed to running a paper mill, a bookbindery, a newspaper chain, and bookstores. He printed many hundreds of titles, from "Goody Two Shoes" to "Fanny Hill."

The dancing mania had hit Boston, but the ladies were no longer hampered by hoop skirts. The gentlemen were now wearing trousers, or "pantaloons," though Paul, in his sixties, still kept to his "small clothes" and stockings. Boston at last had a theater. Bulfinch built it in 1792, and it opened the following year with an M.C. to see that nobody pelted the actors. Boston was well on its way to vaudeville, opera, and X-rated movies.

Boston also had a fine new State House designed by Bulfinch, next to Hancock House on the "governor's pasture." The cornerstone had been laid on July 4, 1795, pulled into place by fifteen white horses representing the fifteen United States, and the aging Sam Adams made the dedicatory speech. Under the cornerstone was put a silver plate, describing the day's ceremonies; guns were fired; and Paul knew he would get a personal report on the building's progress, as one of his sons-in-law was the master builder. But why should not he himself provide the sheet copper for the dome . . .?

Another speech was made, this one by Paul to his fellow Masons, and in it he stated that this was a "Country distinguished from the rest of the world by being a government of Laws, where Liberty has found a safe and secure abode . . ."

From the Fenway

North End

Prudential Tower

Back Bay

Beacon Hill

Athenaeum

Charles River

Antique shop

North End

As We Are Now

What should a city be? Let us consider a few ideal criteria. It should be pleasant and safe to live in, and to get about in. We would have to assume clean air, water, streets, parks, good mass transit, public conveyances, and law-abiding citizens. In fact, a city should receive that loving care so many of us lavish on our houses, lawns, and cars. A city should be spacious and intimate, crowded and uncrowded, simple and complex. There should be easy availability of theater, art, music, dance, and sports. Most important of all, these elements should be set in an ongoing museum, containing the past and the present, filled with harmonious and interesting aesthetic relationships, to give the city dweller, and the visitor, delight for his senses, and also to make him aware of his place in the continuum of human achievement. In this context achievement means pursuit of a quality of life evoked by our most humane and creative ideals.

How well does Boston fit into this idealized picture? Well, at the present time, relative to other cities, it is not doing too badly. Boston has a number of great advantages, of which the most important may be that it is not yet swarming with so many people as to make it unmanageable. Its identity is still intact and still graceful, though cruelly slashed by expressways, those ill-conceived short-term solutions to long-term problems. There are good things left undisturbed, either by accident or by design. There is fresh thinking being done, combined with new directions taken, so that the possibility remains of overcoming hard-core neglect, and the city's potential destruction by rank overgrowth of building, traffic, and population, might still possibly be allayed.

As for safety from street crime, our urban concentrations tend to reflect the climate of our society; so until that climate improves, always with

Parking lot exit

us will be the muggers, the desperate, the neglected; those addicted to the cult of violence; those addicted to the cult of drug nirvana; and those bereft of purpose and direction.

What this discussion is really about is the concept of the model city. Toronto, with which I am slightly familiar, strikes me as being one, in some important aspects. There is a civic pride manifest in the cleanliness of its streets and public transportation, in the care of its buildings, and in the evident and unusual lack of tension, in a multi racial, polyglot city. Toronto has strong indigenous, but unghettoed, neighborhoods, and lacks any area that could be called a slum. Most important in this less than sweet approach to the last quarter of the twentieth century, is the wonderful sense of being able to walk the streets at night without apprehension. No doubt Toronto has its problems, but the atmosphere of civil care is such a fine example of what is possible, that hope is reenforced for the future of civilization.

Why not attempt the development of Boston as America's model city? We could frankly borrow, from cities the world over, concepts that have already proved their worth. Boston, having a central place in our history, is the emotional and logical choice for a demonstration of what cities of the future could be. It has already made progress in this direction, in some of its new planning and rehabilitation, and in the sane preservation of its older architectural forms.

What qualities does Boston already have that can serve as guideposts to a better philosophy of urban planning? It might be well to look at those neighborhoods that give us hints on the directions we might take, as well as some to avoid.

To experience what is meant by diversity within harmony, human scale, the use of warmth and texture in building materials, and pleasure in the creation and viewing of ornament, everyone should be able to walk through Beacon Hill and the Back Bay. They were, essentially, dreams for the Athens of America. Viewing them should be part of the curriculum of every planner, builder, and architect, though we are not suggesting the construction of endless Beacon Hills and Back Bays. This hypothetical walk might just move the builders of the future to impregnate their cold concrete with color. It might teach something about architectural surprises, the value of attempting to build to a more human proportion, and the use of greenery (aside from plastic plants in the lobby).

The impression one is left with, after viewing Beacon Hill and the Back Bay, is the singular one that it is rather difficult to find anything built in the twentieth century with such a symmetrical orchestration of architecture and land. The disharmony in much of our twentieth century building cannot be entirely due to nostalgia for our cultural past, but must also grow out of our disenchantment with the sterile, cold structures erected today. They are edifices that cannot be justified by the rationale of efficiency, for our commercial high-rise is profligate in the use of energy, with a misguided design principle that people should be hermetically enclosed. Strangely enough, some of our more forward-looking architects are rediscovering the opening window! They find that even in high-rise buildings, windows can be designed to louvre in such a way that they achieve ventilation (without blowing all that essential paperwork off the desk), provide shade, and weather protection as well. This raises the thought that it might be highly profitable for us to reappraise many of our old ways of doing things, and see if we can reapply them, albeit improved and shaped to our needs.

From Beacon Hill and the Common it is a natural downhill walk to the Public Garden, which until 1859 was just another bit of swampy, unprofitable land from which the city created a formal garden. And formal it was, with symmetrical plantings, labeled trees, a pond, swanboats, "keep off the grass" signs, and everything as carefully cultivated as Boston society.

Though conventional, the Garden has a remarkably organic flow of paths, following serpentine shores graced by weeping willows, under which, despite the signs, figures still sit and lie on the grass in the classic poses of our early prints. Here in the Garden we begin to realize that Boston was also fertile ground for statues. They are not only the usual monuments to politicians and military men, but venerations in stone to those who left their marks upon the culture of Boston—scholars, poets, writers, artists, abolitionists, explorers, and religionists. Statuary is generally a lost form of city art today. Though some of it is kitsch, much of it, especially in Boston, is finely honed and expressive, lending a nobility of sorts to the urban landscape, and giving the pigeons a safe place to rest. Please, revampers of our cities! Fill our plazas, malls, and parks with sculpture, in keeping with the concept of the city as an open museum, and generate full employment for our artists.

Boston statuary is one of the most engaging aspects of the city, and continues from the Garden all the way along the beautifully tree-shaded Commonwealth Mall. This mall is part of Frederick Law Olmsted's green-belt design ("The emerald necklace") that was to have continuity all the way from the Public Garden up to the Mall, to the Fenway, Jamaicaway, the Arnold Arboretum, and Franklin Park. Well, it still exists, though badly severed by the requirements of the automobile, the

Beacon Street
at the Public Garden

Beacon Hill Lady

*View from
Beacon Hill*

Potwasher

Bookseller

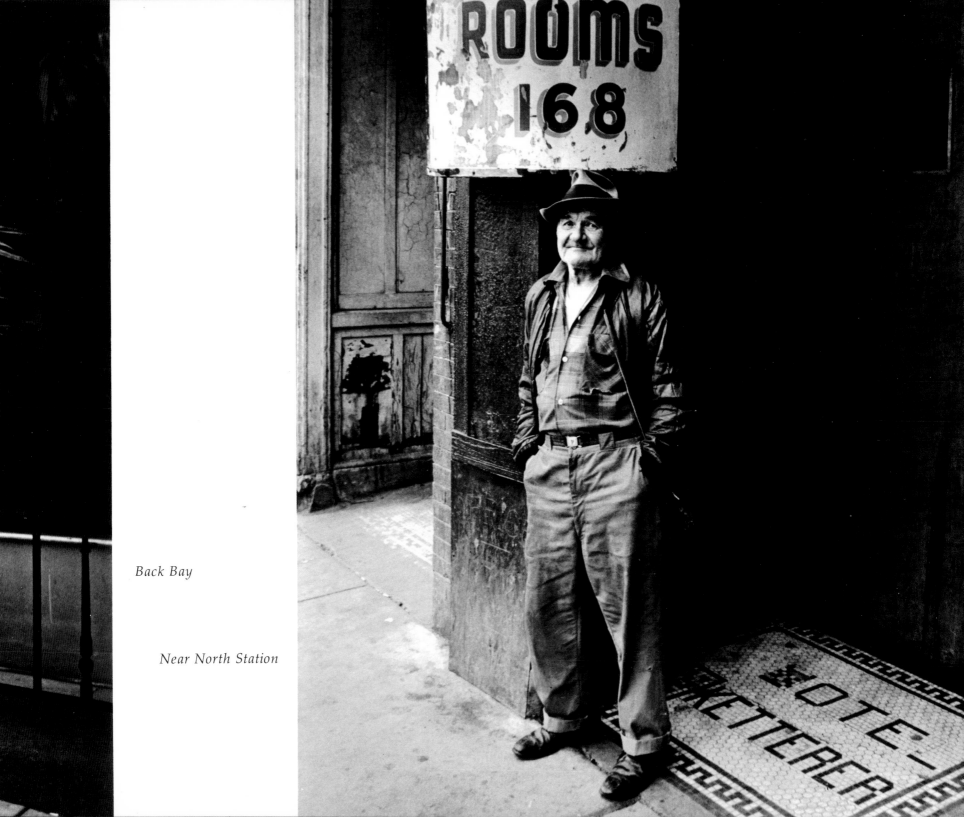

Back Bay

Near North Station

Girl, East Boston

Shoeshine boy, Combat Zone

general heedlessness of modern urban construction, and the exercise of the design principle that cities are built to accommodate cars, not people.

Of all our streets, Commonwealth Avenue, with its central mall, has the spaciousness of a Parisian boulevard, and is a buffer against the invasion of traffic cacophony, and so retains some of its original leisurely atmosphere.

But let us consider one of our attractive, but less fortunate streets. Newbury, which runs parallel to Commonwealth, is really a very pleasant place to browse, with the art galleries, the craft shops, elegant emporia for the well-heeled, and its outdoor cafés, though these are a bit hazed over with exhaust, since the street is throttled with traffic. If any place needs to be converted into a pedestrian mall, it is Newbury Street, which begs to be freed of the automobiles, at least for the five blocks starting at the Public Garden. The general need for auto-free malls is not being met in Boston. The car still has a stranglehold on the city, and that condition will persist until we initiate new ways to garage, away from our pleasanter streets, those that *must* come to the city. In this respect the under-the-Common garage was a fine idea, except for the architectural banalities that are the entry and exit buildings, scattered over the landscape of the lower Common. If only they were the public johns they appear to be! An indication of how civilized a city or country is (in the amenities at least), and its awareness of the human physiology, is the number of its clean, spacious, cared-for "public conveniences," and I am literally pained to relate that Boston and the U.S. utterly fail here. In contrast, the British Isles is a jewel of western civilization.

There *are* ways of solving urban traffic problems. How about some new-old ideas, like an extensive urban trolley system, with sides open in summer? Remember? How about little electric go-abouts, like the ones Amsterdam is experimenting with? How about enticing people to reach the city with plentiful and attractive public transport?

We have digressed. The sun can still shine into Newbury Street, for the buildings are late nineteenth, early twentieth century low-rise. There is a different façade on every building; and it is a very worthwhile street in which to look upward, to see the many rooflines, the window shapes, and the art of stonework, lovingly done when there seemed still to be time and inclination for the decoration of our commercial and public buildings. Newbury Street is a charming sample of the complicated structures of that era. There are quaint American interpretations of Gothic, Rococo, Renaissance, ancient Greek, and art deco styles, giving birth to all kinds of strange hybrids, some of them quite delightful and original. You will find them everywhere in the older commercial districts of Boston—Washington and Tremont streets, Milk, State, Battery and Broad—just raise your eyes. These buildings deserve to be with us for a long time, and there is no reason why they should not; some of them look as solid as the pyramids. We certainly will never build their like again, though this virtue has not saved them from being torn down in the past, and often replaced by that architectural marvel, the parking lot. There is a renewed hope for their continued existence, however, due to today's building costs. Refurbishing the old might well be more economical than tearing them down and building anew.

Only one block over from Newbury Street is Copley Square, surrounded by the strong period pieces of Trinity Church, the Copley Plaza Hotel, and the Public Library. The library has one of the most charming inner courts anywhere, providing a

India Street

108

Haymarket Station

Bridge,
Charles River Dam

Hotel Porter

Charlestown

*Isabella Stewart
Gardner Museum*

Court Street

Gentleman at New City Hall

Schoolteacher

At Trinity Church
Forest Hills Cemetery ▶

· PHILLIPS · BROOKS ·
PREACHER · OF · THE · WORD · OF · GOD
LOVER · OF · MANKIND
BORN · IN · BOSTON · A·D · MDCCCXXXV
DIED · IN · BOSTON · A·D · MDCCCXCIII
THIS · MONVMENT · IS · ERECTED · BY
HIS · FELLOW · CITIZENS · A·D · MCMX

Detail, Somerset Street

place to rest and read in plant-filled shade. The foliage- and flower-filled court should be reconsidered when we have to build new public buildings, as it just might give bureaucracy a more amiable center. Even in modern office buildings it is valid, if only as a place to have a pleasant lunch, and to sit in the sun, and recover from office routine.

The Plaza itself, redesigned a few years ago, was a revamping that ended up as an acre of concrete, that is subarctic in the winter, and fries in the summer, when it is partially saved by a large fountain of rather sterile design, that cools things in the immediate vicinity. There is a small planting of trees alongside Trinity Church, which helps, but the meagre sitting space in the Plaza consists of molded concrete that never seems to match the temperature of the human posterior. I suppose it is another sign of the times. The use of wooden benches is precluded by today's vandalism—or they say it is. But I still think "they" could have tried wood slats imbedded in concrete ends, and more benches, and more plantings, and some color design in the stone. As it is, the general impression is arid.

Looming over the Plaza is the new Hancock Building, an obtrusive object lesson in building technology, constructed without adequate research into its possible future impact. In this particular case, the immediate future, as its windows started to fall out almost as soon as they were put in. Now, after almost two years, "they" say that this problem is being solved. I hope so, for without the reflecting effect of its windows this would just be another overwhelming slab of modern high-rise. This huge mirror that reflects Trinity Church and the moving sky can be rather spectacular, and so somewhat compensates for the fact that the whole concept is out of scale.

Just beyond Copley Plaza is that no man's land of depressing railway overpasses and expressway exits that leads us into the neglect of the South End and Roxbury. The South End still sustains some of the elegance of its past, with bow-front windows and mansard roofs, and with some streets opening up to contained little parks protected with wrought-iron fences. A fair number of these houses have been saved from terminal neglect by new people moving in and rehabilitating these once lovely dwellings, with some beneficial effect on the immediate neighborhood. The South End has had some piecemeal urban renewal, some of it not too bad, and some huge public housing conglomerations, which are joyless welfare cubicles. Skid Row resides here, and as a whole, the area needs rehabilitation, and the building up of a solid, self-aware community.

Roxbury, despite urban renewal efforts that have had some measure of success, is still one of our most depressed areas. A ghetto for the Irish in 1850, then for the Jews and blacks toward the end of the nineteenth century, Roxbury is now almost entirely for blacks, whose isolation stretches well into Mattapan. Here the islands of urban renewal still sit in a sea of decay. The area is a reminder of the American sickness, racism; until the national conscience and imagination are fired to move toward an enormous and necessary urban rebuilding project (which, God knows, should start with our Harlems and Roxburys), the social barriers cannot be torn down between Americans as human beings. Any process of building livable environments out of the neglect they now live in should deeply involve the inhabitants. This is the only way to generate work and pride in their own community. Idealistic? Yes, but we must ask if there is any other way in which cities can survive. We display a rather terrifying obtuse-

ness as to where the real self-interest of America lies. There can be no doubt that the longer we delay in doing something, the more insoluble becomes the problem.

Now let us take a look at some nice places we do have: City Hall Plaza, for one—and let us note how we have spent our money there. Rather well: the plaza has a spaciousness that never seems to fill, and it allows one to view the surrounding city from an open perspective that is panoramic, with much of architectural interest. The graceful curves of Sears' Crescent have been successfully repeated by the center plaza, and the Crescent has been nicely rehabilitated, with an open air, exhaust-free restaurant at its base. The New City Hall is really monumental, its cast concrete broken by interesting facing, done in the traditional red brick of Boston, though some of its deep open recesses lack light and have the look of having never been trod by man or beast since it was built. Taken together it is a building that intrigues, and if you walk up its ramps to look about you, it creates a frame that complements the view. The Plaza itself has a rather fine stepped waterfall that encourages one to linger, watch, and let the endless flow smooth out whatever has churned you up lately—a convenient form of mental hydrotherapy. There are potted trees on one side, but again there is a vast area of gray concrete that still needs some warmth.

Most of old Boston lies on the waterfront side of City Hall, and visible are Faneuil Hall, Quincy Market, and a row of old commercial buildings that are being restored. Then the eye is halted by the ugly disruption of the central artery (the expressway), behind which is hidden the North End. Faneuil Hall and Quincy Market still partly function in their old manner. There are political meetings and forums at the Hall, and Quincy Market still

Charlestown

houses active markets that handle a variety of commodities, from meat to flowers. The whole area is thriving much as it always has, and this is precisely what keeps this part of historical Boston alive. By all means we should venerate the symbols of our history, but it is equally important that community life continues in and around them.

From the end of the market district a mercifully short walk through the cruddy underbelly of the expressway bridge brings us into the North End, the home of Paul Revere, the Old North Church, Copp's Hill Burying Ground and the Italian community of Boston. Now it is tangible that we are in a place that is self-contained, and for the moment secure in the traditions of its culture (at least for the older generations residing there, who are not tucked away in cubic container care). Paul Revere Mall is as notable for its view of older Italians busy with games and talk, as it is for its view of the night rider statue, and the Old North Church. Whatever its problems, the North End is of a piece, with the smells of pastry and bread, and language flowing between people who still see each other as part of a community. Tenements and grubby streets, yes, but a neighborhood infinitely preferable to the atomization of most apartment high-rise.

A city is neighborhoods, all with a different stamp and purpose. Neighborhoods, even while they have their own strong characters, must also have the assurance that they can intermingle with benefit to all. Boston is still a place where this can happen, though some of the communities are being fractured, and to the extent that they are, they are less pleasant places to live in. Solutions to our cities' problems that aim at total homogenization of a population tucked away in high-rise, towering over dead streets, will not be the way Boston goes, will it?

127